EPHEMERIS OF PLANETARY STELLAR CONJUNCTIONS

2025

Adrian Buonaparte

CONTENTS

INTRODUCTION

The fixed stars hold significant importance due to their enduring positions and profound influence on natal, horary and electional charts. Unlike the wandering planets, fixed stars remain in constant positions relative to the celestial sphere, providing a stable reference point. Each fixed star is associated with specific qualities and mythologies, which can deeply affect an individual's character and life events when they align with key points in the natal chart, such as the Ascendant, Midheaven, or the planets.

For example, the fixed star Regulus, known as the "Heart of the Lion," is traditionally associated with royalty, honour, and courage. When prominently positioned in a natal chart, it can indicate a person destined for leadership and recognition. Similarly, the fixed star Algol is often linked with intense emotional experiences and transformative challenges.

Astrologers use the fixed stars to add depth and nuance to their interpretations, offering insights into hidden talents, potential pitfalls, and the overall destiny of an individual. Understanding the influence of fixed stars enriches the practice of astrology, providing a more comprehensive and detailed analysis of one's astrological profile.

To my knowledge, this is the first time that an Ephemeris of planetary conjunctions with the fixed stars has been published in the English language for Western astrology.

Apart from the Sun, Moon and planets, these tables also include the North Node. In this edition I have excluded the asteroids, but may consider them in future editions.

This work is limited to Bernadette Brady's fixed stars, as these were deemed to be most important, as described in her major book on this subject. No doubt there are innumerable others, but these have not as yet been well delineated in the astrological literature. Research in this field is ongoing, and future issues will incorporate them as more information emerges.

To facilitate searches and for convenience, there are tables listing the stars in alphabetical order, zodiac longitude order and also declination order. The values for both the tropical zodiac and the sidereal (Lahiri) zodiac are given.

All the times shown in the tables are for UTC (GMT). The reader will need to make appropriate adjustments according to their time zones. All calculations were made using the electional search facility of the Solar Fire astrology software, and hence their accuracy is limited by this program.

TRADITIONAL INSIGHTS ON THE FIXED STARS

In astrology, fixed stars have long been considered powerful symbols that offer insight into a person's character, fate, and spiritual inclinations. Classical astrologers, including Ptolemy and Al-Biruni, categorized stars according to their unique qualities, often linking them with planets to better understand their influence. In Ptolemy's Tetrabiblos, he associates stars with planetary qualities; for instance, Sirius carries Mars-Jupiter attributes, contributing an intense and ambitious nature, while Spica is linked to Venus-Mars, bestowing talents and charisma. Al-Biruni also notes that fixed stars bring depth to the natal chart, marking qualities that can influence life direction and spiritual growth.

When closely conjunct personal planets or angles (such as the Ascendant or Midheaven), fixed stars can add intense, sometimes fated qualities to one's personality and life path. For example, Regulus on the Ascendant suggests leadership and prominence, yet warns against pride.

Medieval astrologers saw these stars as influencing specific areas of life or even body parts; Algol, often associated with misfortune, was linked to the head and neck in medical astrology. Renaissance astrologers expanded on these meanings, seeing fixed stars as markers of ambition, skill, or spiritual insight depending on their constellation and characteristics.

The following is a summary of the traditional interpretations of Brady's 60 fixed stars. These are mostly based on the ancient Greek, Arabic and Medieval classic texts.

Achernar

Achernar, also known as α Eridani, is a fixed star located at the mouth of the celestial river Eridanus. Its name derives from the Arabic "Al Ahir," meaning "the end of the river." Achernar is traditionally associated with the beneficial qualities of Jupiter, with an added Mars-Uranus influence, which lends a dynamic, sometimes intense nature. This star is often interpreted as symbolizing success, philosophical inclinations, and religious devotion. It brings qualities like patience, industriousness, and honours, particularly in public roles and positions within religious institutions.

When well-aspected, Achernar is believed to bring happiness, moral integrity, and faithfulness to one's beliefs. This Jupiter-like influence suggests a tendency toward generosity, spirituality, and beneficence, making it favourable for those seeking or holding public office. Furthermore, Achernar is noted to rule the centre of the left foot in medical astrology, indicating potential influences on that area.

Acrux

The fixed star Acrux (α Crucis), located in the Southern Cross constellation, is known for its potent and spiritual significance. Its nature blends the influences of Jupiter and Mars, which together bestow courage, strength, and a pronounced spiritual or philosophical inclination. Acrux is often associated with intellectual and religious pursuits, supporting qualities like wisdom, dedication, and a strong moral compass.

This star is particularly linked to people who engage in spiritual or religious leadership, showing an inclination toward practices that guide or serve others. Acrux's energy encourages a deep sense of commitment to higher principles, fostering attributes such as loyalty, honour, and a desire for justice. When prominent in an astrological chart, it may bring success through teaching, healing, or service-based professions, where individuals are guided by ethical values and spiritual dedication.

Acrux is also said to influence the feet in medical astrology, potentially symbolizing a grounding energy that connects physical action with higher ideals. Its Jupiter-Mars mix implies an active pursuit of goals, often driven by a personal philosophy or belief system that motivates disciplined and purposeful actions. Those influenced by Acrux might find themselves drawn to roles that integrate authority with service, or where they can apply their values in practical ways to effect change or provide guidance.

Acrux's influence is generally positive, enhancing spiritual depth and moral integrity while supporting ambitions tied to learning, teaching, and leadership. Its alignment in a chart can indicate a path of service or dedication to meaningful causes, grounded in a philosophy of justice and wisdom.

Acubens

The fixed star Acubens, located in the constellation Cancer (α Cancri), carries a Mars-Mercury influence. This star is associated with a sharp intellect, resilience, and a defensive or protective quality, often connected to the "claw" of the crab, which signifies both grasping and guarding attributes. Those under Acubens' influence may demonstrate keen mental agility and strategic thinking, often excelling in areas where problem-solving and adaptability are required. Acubens may also point to a tendency toward secrecy or holding private information, reflecting Cancer's protective nature. While it can enhance analytical abilities and persistence, it also brings the potential for defensiveness or a guarded approach to personal and professional matters. This star is sometimes associated with surgical skills or hands-on abilities due to the precision implied by its Mars-Mercury mix, benefiting careers in medicine or technical fields.

In health-related astrology, Acubens is sometimes linked to issues with the hands or arms, areas ruled by Mercury. Its influence can also manifest in a strong desire for freedom and independence, which may lead to resisting constraints or limitations. Generally, Acubens supports a quick, inventive mind paired with a determined spirit, helping individuals navigate challenging situations with resourcefulness and a protective sense of self.

Aculeus

This star, located in the constellation Scorpio, is associated with intensity, endurance, and overcoming hardship. Known for its close connection with the star Acumen, Aculeus represents the "stinger" or thorn of the Scorpion and is tied to challenges or difficulties that, when faced, can lead to personal growth and resilience. This star embodies a Mars-Moon influence, giving those under its sway a fearless or sometimes combative nature, as well as a profound ability to endure adversity.

Aculeus' placement in a chart can highlight areas of struggle, particularly those that test one's patience, courage, and persistence. Individuals with strong Aculeus influences may encounter criticism, opposition, or obstacles that ultimately serve as catalysts for strength and transformation. Aculeus also has associations with vision and perception, potentially influencing one's insights and mental clarity when under pressure.

In medical astrology, Aculeus is linked to vision and eyesight. This star's energy may lead individuals to situations that require them to see beyond surface appearances, sometimes experiencing literal or metaphorical "blurriness" before achieving a clearer perspective. Overall, Aculeus invites one to embrace challenges as opportunities for growth, fostering resilience and a deeper understanding of life's struggles.

Acumen

Acumen, located in the "sting" of Scorpio, is symbolically linked to themes of endurance, hardship, and resilience. Like its companion star Aculeus, Acumen's energy is associated with facing and overcoming challenges. This star is often described as having a Mars-Moon influence, which can make individuals with strong Acumen placements in their charts bold, persistent, and sometimes confrontational. Acumen's influence suggests that those under its sway may encounter periods of difficulty, criticism, or opposition. However, these experiences are often transformative, strengthening one's character and ability to handle adversity.

Acumen is associated with vision and perception, particularly with a "blurred" or obstructed view, which can reflect both literal and metaphorical blindness that one overcomes through experience and perseverance. In medical astrology, Acumen, like Aculeus, is linked to eyesight issues, symbolizing a need to develop clarity in difficult situations. Thus, Acumen represents the theme of achieving insight and resilience through trials, rewarding persistence with a deeper understanding of self and others.

Agena

Agena, also known as Beta Centauri, holds astrological significance as a star associated with themes of commitment, loyalty, and purposeful action. Located in the constellation of Centaurus, Agena carries a strong Venus-Jupiter influence, which is seen to offer abundance, generosity, and success, especially in partnerships and social interactions. This combination promotes a harmonious and compassionate nature, often linked to deep connections, love for family, and a protective quality toward others.

It can enhance one's natural charisma and social appeal, making it easier for those with a prominent Agena placement in their natal charts to attract beneficial relationships and alliances. Its influence often brings luck and favor in personal relationships and can support individuals in roles where cooperation and diplomacy are key. There is also an element of healing and guidance in Agena's symbolism, potentially marking those under its influence as mentors or nurturing figures within their communities.

However, the star's influence requires a balance, as its energy can sometimes lead to excess or overindulgence if not moderated. When positively aligned, Agena is considered to bring honour and respect, success in partnerships, and the ability to inspire others through kindness and strong moral values.

Alcyone

Alcyone, the brightest star in the Pleiades cluster, is renowned in astrology for its intense and sometimes challenging influence. It has a nature similar to Mars and the Moon, representing both ambition and emotion. Alcyone often embodies themes of wisdom, vision, and action, marking those influenced by it as driven, highly perceptive, and sometimes controversial figures. This star is linked to intellectual pursuits, leadership, and the potential to achieve distinction, especially when driven by a sense of purpose or cause.

Astrologically, Alcyone is said to bestow a sense of high ambition and determination but may also create a tendency toward intensity and conflict if misaligned. Traditional interpretations suggest that Alcyone can bring challenges, such as a propensity for strong emotions or moral rigidity, which could lead to confrontations or hardships in relationships. Yet, when well-placed, Alcyone encourages personal growth through overcoming adversity and can reward perseverance with honour and respect. The star's influence on vision, both literal and symbolic, often connects with those interested in mystical or spiritual wisdom, and it is seen as an indicator of strong intuition and insight.

Those with a significant placement of Alcyone in their charts may also experience a deep emotional resonance with matters of social justice, philosophy, or spiritual evolution, often feeling called to act on their convictions.

Aldebaran

Aldebaran, one of the brightest stars in the night sky, is a significant fixed star in astrology, associated with qualities of honour, ambition, and martial strength. Often referred to as the "Watcher of the East," it marks the eye of the bull in the constellation Taurus. Its energy is likened to that of Mars, imparting courage, leadership qualities, and an active spirit. Aldebaran's influence is frequently linked with a strong drive for success and power, making it favourable for pursuits that require determination and resilience.

Astrologically, Aldebaran is considered a "Royal Star," which traditionally grants protection and success but also carries warnings. Its positive influence can bestow high social status, wealth, and respect, often supporting those in leadership roles or military endeavours. However, the star's energy requires maintaining integrity and moral principles; when misused, Aldebaran's energy may lead to downfall or scandal, highlighting the need for ethical behaviour to sustain its blessings.

In natal charts, Aldebaran is often associated with visionary qualities, assertiveness, and the potential for significant accomplishments, especially when conjunct the Sun, Moon, or prominent planets. Its influence on health is sometimes connected to the throat and neck area, due to its placement in Taurus. This star encourages individuals to pursue their goals with fortitude while heeding the consequences of unethical actions, blending ambition with an emphasis on integrity.

Algol

Algol, also known as the "Demon Star," is one of the most infamous fixed stars in astrology. Located in the constellation Perseus, this binary star has been linked with themes of intense power, transformation, and challenges, often associated with drastic changes, sudden losses, or situations involving dark, intense energies. Astrologically, Algol represents primal, untamed forces and is considered a powerful yet difficult influence, demanding a balanced approach to navigate its energy positively.

Algol's reputation stems partly from its association with Medusa, the mythical figure who could turn people to stone with her gaze. Similarly, in a natal chart, Algol is believed to bring both risk and potential for significant personal evolution if one can overcome or channel its intense forces. Traditionally, Algol is said to bring dangers or misfortune when activated, but contemporary interpretations suggest it can also empower individuals to face life's darker aspects and emerge resilient.

When well-aspected, Algol can foster resilience, depth, and the ability to confront and transform adversity into strength. However, it emphasizes the need to handle power responsibly. In medical astrology, Algol is linked with the throat and neck area, and some interpretations suggest it might indicate vulnerabilities in these areas if negatively aspected. Algol's placement in a chart or by transit may indicate times of intense emotional or psychological trials, but with the potential for profound transformation and healing if approached with awareness and integrity.

Alhena

Alhena, a bright star in the constellation Gemini, is known in astrology for its associations with artistry, eloquence, and spiritual insight. Often called the "Proudly Marching One," Alhena is located on the left foot of the Gemini twins, symbolizing both movement and direction. Its astrological influence is traditionally linked to qualities of intellectual prowess, creativity, and a strong sense of purpose, particularly in matters related to communication, the arts, and healing.

it is said to impart a love of beauty, refinement, and a talent for expressing one's thoughts clearly. Individuals influenced by Alhena often have a sense of mission and may be driven to share their insights or artistic creations with the world. Positively aspected, Alhena can bring success in writing, music, and art, along with a reputation for integrity and insight. However, when negatively aspected, it may indicate challenges in expressing oneself or an inclination toward pride or stubbornness.

In terms of health and body symbolism, Alhena is linked with the ankles and feet, and its placement in a chart may hint at strengths or vulnerabilities in these areas. Overall, Alhena represents the merging of intellectual gifts with creative or spiritual purpose, encouraging those it influences to pursue a path of personal expression aligned with higher ideals.

Alkes

The fixed star Alkes, located in the constellation Crater, represents the concept of a "vessel" or "cup" and is traditionally associated with vitality, knowledge, and preservation. Alkes conveys a strong sense of purpose and continuity, symbolizing the passing of knowledge or a legacy, often in a manner aligned with protection or guardianship. This star is connected to qualities of reliability, honour, and an enduring impact, making it favourable for those in roles involving teaching, healing, or any work requiring dedication and care for future generations.

Alkes is seen as a star of strength and durability, helping individuals to carry on traditions or principles, much like a vessel that holds and protects. Individuals influenced by

Alkes may feel called to conserve resources, uphold standards, or protect valuable knowledge or people. This sense of preservation and guardianship can inspire these individuals to work diligently within family structures, educational fields, or in roles involving environmental or societal preservation.

When positively aspected, Alkes can enhance a person's determination, resilience, and ability to nurture something of value over time. However, if negatively influenced, it may lead to rigidity or an overly cautious nature that resists necessary changes. Overall, Alkes symbolizes the preservation of wisdom and continuity across generations, encouraging dedication to causes that benefit future progress and stability.

Alnilam

In astrology, Alnilam, a prominent star in Orion's Belt, is known for its association with clarity, ambition, and transformation. Known as one of the "Three Kings" or "Three Sisters," Alnilam holds significant influence, often compared to the expansive, optimistic qualities of Jupiter. It is believed to grant inspiration, leadership ability, and a drive for excellence, especially in intellectual or creative pursuits. Those influenced by Alnilam may possess strong vision and determination, finding themselves driven by high aspirations and a sense of purpose.

The star's energy is also associated with themes of truth-seeking and personal growth, helping individuals align with deeper self-understanding or spiritual goals. When well-aspected, Alnilam can lend focus, clarity, and resilience in overcoming obstacles, often guiding one toward enlightenment or profound knowledge. However, if negatively influenced, it might bring struggles with pride, rigidity, or detachment, as individuals may find themselves overly focused on ideals or ambitions at the expense of balance in their personal lives.

Alnilam's influence is ideal for those in positions requiring insight, creativity, or leadership, especially in fields such as education, spirituality, or the arts. Overall, it represents a journey of self-mastery, encouraging ambition, wisdom, and a pursuit of higher truths.

Alphard

This is the principal star in the constellation Hydra, is symbolically rich and associated with emotional intensity, inner strength, and sometimes challenging life experiences.

Known as the "Heart of the Serpent," this fixed star has connections to themes of passion, impulsive emotions, and self-control. It carries a Mars-Saturn nature, which can lead to turbulent or deeply transformative energies. Alphard is associated with resilience and the capacity to navigate complex emotional landscapes, as well as to overcome adversities, especially those linked to relationships, personal desires, or ethical dilemmas.

Alphard's influence can manifest as a drive to explore emotional depths and maintain integrity, often through situations that test one's will or moral compass. It encourages introspection and may foster a sense of spiritual or personal independence. For those who can channel Alphard's energy constructively, it can bestow leadership qualities and a determined approach to personal growth. However, if negatively aspected, it may amplify tendencies toward jealousy, impulsiveness, or even self-destruction, requiring individuals to cultivate patience and self-discipline.

Those with Alphard prominent in their charts may be drawn to healing or transformation-focused fields, as the star is linked to a profound understanding of the complexities of the human experience. Astrologically, it serves as both a warning and a guide, emphasizing the importance of mastering inner emotions and making conscientious choices in life.

Alphecca

Alphecca, located in the constellation Corona Borealis, is symbolically tied to creativity, beauty, and a strong sense of honour. Alphecca, sometimes called Gemma, holds a Venus-Mercury nature, bestowing qualities like artistic talent, refinement, and charm. Individuals with Alphecca prominent in their chart often have a flair for the arts and communication, reflecting an attraction to beauty and elegance in life.

Astrologically, Alphecca is associated with personal achievements and the promise of success, especially in creative or artistic endeavours. It brings a desire for recognition and a need to establish an individual identity. Though it often conveys good fortune, Alphecca also brings challenges; it emphasizes the necessity of maintaining integrity, as temptations or lapses in ethics may lead to struggles. Traditional texts note that this star offers both material and spiritual gifts, though it may present trials that test one's values.

Alphecca's influence is particularly potent when conjunct significant planets, potentially amplifying its effects of charm and artistic inclination. Those under its influence may also find themselves in roles of responsibility or positions that attract public attention. This star's energy fosters a sense of inner pride and encourages self-expression, making it a notable symbol for those engaged in the pursuit of artistic or personal mastery.

Alpheraz

The fixed star Alpheraz (also known as Sirrah or Alpha Andromedae) resides in the Andromeda constellation and is traditionally linked to themes of independence, freedom, and strength of character. Alpheraz is associated with a Venus-Jupiter influence, which brings social grace, charm, and the potential for personal success. Those with Alpheraz prominent in their chart may exhibit qualities of confidence, beauty, and social magnetism, often attracting favourable attention in social or artistic circles.

Alpheraz's energy can provide a liberating force, helping individuals break free from restrictions and pursue their own goals, aligning with Andromeda's myth of breaking from chains. The star promotes leadership and assertiveness while encouraging personal freedom, which can be particularly beneficial in pursuits that require self-confidence and expression. Traditionally, it is thought to grant a degree of protection or good fortune, especially in social and financial matters.

Conjunctions with planets such as the Sun or Moon can amplify Alpheraz's influence, enhancing social status, popularity, and a sense of well-being. Alpheraz's energy favours harmony and charisma, making it beneficial in professions involving public relations, entertainment, or any field where interpersonal connections are key.

Al Rischa

The fixed star Al Rischa, located in the constellation Pisces, represents the knot tying the two fish in the mythological story of Pisces. Astrologically, Al Rischa is often associated with connections, union, and spiritual links, symbolizing bonds that unify separate elements or paths. This star's name derives from the Arabic word for "the cord" or "knot," reinforcing its thematic emphasis on unification and continuity.

Al Rischa carries a Mercury-Saturn influence, combining intellectual depth with responsibility and structure. This influence often leads to practicality in communication and wisdom in forming lasting commitments or connections. People with strong alignments to Al Rischa in their charts may have a heightened sense of purpose in relationships, desiring meaning and continuity in partnerships, be they romantic, professional, or spiritual. This star is thought to impart qualities like dependability and commitment, making it beneficial for careers requiring disciplined communication, organization, or mediation skills.

When aligned with the Moon, Sun, or other personal planets, Al Rischa enhances the drive for harmonious relationships and meaningful collaborations, suggesting success in endeavours that rely on cooperation and shared goals. Al Rischa's energy also emphasizes the importance of spiritual growth through connection, aligning the individual's sense of purpose with a broader sense of unity or cosmic order.

Altair

Located in the constellation Aquila ("The Eagle"), Altair is associated with boldness, courage, and a strong drive for freedom. Its influence is marked by a Mars-Jupiter nature, combining assertiveness and ambition (Mars) with a sense of vision, confidence, and expansiveness (Jupiter). Altair is known to endow individuals with qualities of leadership and decisiveness, encouraging them to take calculated risks and act with purpose. This star also often relates to speed, both in physical endeavours and in mental processes, leading to a swift, energetic approach to tasks.

When connected to key planets, Altair can heighten a person's instinct for survival, fostering a "warrior" mindset. This influence is favourable for military or athletic careers, where bravery and quick action are valued. In the realm of personal growth, Altair encourages independence and self-determination, often driving individuals to pursue paths that offer a sense of autonomy and freedom. However, its bold energy may sometimes lead to impulsive or overly ambitious actions if not tempered with caution.

Altair is also associated with sharpness in intellect and expression, making it beneficial for those in fields requiring strategic thinking or persuasive communication. The star's symbolism of the "Eagle" brings themes of far-reaching vision and elevated perspective, often helping individuals cultivate a broader outlook on life or develop long-term goals that align with their higher purpose.

Ankaa

The fixed star Ankaa, located in the constellation Phoenix, is often linked to themes of rebirth, resilience, and transformation, mirroring the mythological phoenix that rises from its ashes. Astrologically, Ankaa is considered to have a combined Mars-Mercury influence, which gives it qualities of intellect, communication, and assertive energy. This star is thought to provide individuals with a resourceful and dynamic nature, often helping them navigate challenges with a strong inner drive and the ability to renew themselves after setbacks.

When in prominent aspects in a natal chart, Ankaa can enhance one's capacity for self-reinvention and may encourage a pursuit of truth or knowledge, particularly in areas that require analytical and pioneering thought. It also fosters independence, and those influenced by Ankaa may be drawn to paths that emphasize originality and self-reliance. In synastry and transits, Ankaa's energy may signify periods of significant change or renewal, urging one to embrace personal growth and transformation.

This star's fiery energy, reminiscent of Mars, can also contribute a boldness and intensity in personality, often supporting one's ability to act decisively. However, it also calls for mindfulness, as its influence may at times lead to impulsiveness if not well-balanced.

Antares

Antares, the fixed star located in the heart of the Scorpius constellation, is known as one of the four royal stars of ancient Persia, representing the "Watcher of the West." It holds a powerful, complex influence in astrology, often associated with themes of intensity, ambition, and confrontation. Its nature combines the qualities of Mars and Jupiter, imparting a bold and fiery energy that emphasizes courage, leadership, and assertiveness.

It is linked to a strong drive for success and recognition, which can bring about both triumphs and conflicts. When prominently placed in a natal chart, it encourages resilience, fearlessness, and the ability to confront challenges head-on. However, this intensity also brings the potential for destructiveness if its energy is not balanced. Antares's influence may drive individuals toward high-stakes pursuits and inspire a desire for transformation, but it warns against excessive pride or ruthlessness, which can lead to adversarial situations.

Traditionally, Antares is seen as a marker of powerful, albeit potentially dangerous, energy, capable of achieving greatness through determination but cautioning against a tendency to go to extremes. In transits, it often signals periods of intense focus on goals and a need to remain adaptable amidst intense situations.

Arcturus

Arcturus, the brightest star in the constellation Boötes, is revered for its powerful, protective energy in astrology. Known as a "guardian" star, Arcturus is symbolized by qualities of guidance, courage, and forward-thinking vision. It combines the influences of Mars and Jupiter, giving it a dynamic, assertive quality while also offering benevolence, wisdom, and an inclination toward social justice.

Astrologically, Arcturus is associated with innovation, originality, and leadership. Individuals with a strong connection to Arcturus in their charts may be driven by progressive ideals and a desire to improve society, often taking on leadership roles or pioneering new paths. It's seen as a guiding star for those who seek to challenge conventional boundaries and uplift others through positive change.

Arcturus is also protective, helping one navigate through difficulties with resilience and a sense of purpose. It's linked to success in adventurous or courageous endeavours and often brings recognition or fame when well-aspected. However, Arcturus can also magnify the drive to succeed and achieve, which may lead to intense ambition or restlessness if not tempered.

In general, Arcturus brings a beneficial influence, encouraging individuals to aspire toward higher principles and to use their energy for constructive purposes.

Bellatrix

Bellatrix, located in the constellation Orion, is known as the "Female Warrior" star and carries a Mars-Mercury influence, combining the assertiveness of Mars with the intellect and adaptability of Mercury. In astrology, Bellatrix is associated with courage, strength, quick thinking, and determination. It's linked to success achieved through hard work and resilience, often favoring individuals who show bravery and an independent spirit.

Those with a prominent Bellatrix placement in their natal charts are often ambitious, assertive, and competitive, qualities that may lead to achievement, particularly in fields requiring determination and mental acuity. The star also symbolizes a warrior-like strength, and its energy may manifest as a sharp, strategic approach to challenges. However, it can also bring an inclination toward impatience or overconfidence, especially when unchecked.

Despite its positive attributes, Bellatrix also has a reputation for bringing abrupt changes or difficulties if not well-aspected, suggesting that its gifts require careful management. Its influence often calls for discipline and focus to harness its power effectively and avoid the pitfalls of recklessness.

Betelgeuse

Betelgeuse, a prominent star in Orion, is known for its striking reddish hue and immense brightness. Astrologically, Betelgeuse is generally associated with Mars and Mercury energies, blending assertive, action-oriented qualities with communication, intellect, and adaptability. This star is often linked to success, especially in military, leadership, or public roles, and is believed to bestow honour, fame, and a positive public image.

For individuals with Betelgeuse strongly positioned in their charts, the star's influence can bring bravery, ambition, and a strong sense of purpose. However, its fiery nature also carries potential volatility. Traditionally, Betelgeuse is known to confer "martial honours," indicating the star's favor toward those who act decisively and fearlessly, even in uncertain or risky situations.

Betelgeuse can also symbolize endurance and adaptability. Its presence is considered fortuitous in competitive fields but also warns against impulsivity and rash decisions. Those influenced by Betelgeuse are often advised to channel its bold energy thoughtfully, using it for constructive pursuits. When positively aspected, Betelgeuse's influence brings courage, quick wit, and recognition, while challenging aspects might amplify conflicts or power struggles.

Canopus

Canopus, the second-brightest star in the night sky, is associated with guidance, leadership, and wisdom in astrology. Positioned in the constellation Carina, Canopus embodies Jupiter-like qualities and, to a lesser extent, Saturn's influence, granting authority, respect, and influence, particularly to those in high positions or involved in navigation or discovery. Its influence has historically symbolized protection and acts as a "beacon" or "guiding light" for voyagers and seekers of truth.

Individuals with Canopus strongly positioned in their charts often possess a deep sense of responsibility, wisdom, and a natural ability to lead or advise. In particular, Canopus' connection to Jupiter confers an optimistic outlook, encouraging the individual to seek knowledge and enlightenment. The star's association with navigation aligns it with a drive for exploration, which can be intellectual, spiritual, or physical. It often benefits those in positions where wise judgment is essential, such as advisors, philosophers, or explorers.

Though generally favourable, Canopus also brings a cautionary note when negatively aspected, as it may magnify challenges in maintaining one's principles under pressure or avoiding moral compromises. In its most positive form, Canopus promotes integrity, respect for knowledge, and a balanced approach to authority.

Capella

Located in the constellation Auriga, Capella is a bright star associated with nurturing, protective, and leadership qualities. In astrology, Capella combines the influence of

Mars and Mercury, symbolizing a bold yet strategic energy. It is often linked to curiosity, a desire for knowledge, and a pioneering spirit, making it favourable for those involved in intellectual pursuits, travel, or exploration.

Capella's influence brings courage, determination, and a quick mind, enhancing the ability to navigate complex situations effectively. Those with Capella prominent in their chart may possess a natural inclination toward leadership, often in fields that require both insight and assertiveness. However, its Martian influence can introduce impulsiveness if not balanced by its Mercurial side, which emphasizes communication and adaptability.

Traditionally, Capella is also connected with a protective energy, likened to a guardian that supports those who take calculated risks and uphold integrity. When well-aspected, Capella can bring opportunities for success, recognition, and intellectual accomplishment. In challenging aspects, it may indicate struggles with impulsiveness or impatience. Overall, Capella bestows a dynamic and pioneering influence that favours individuals who pursue their goals with both intellect and bravery.

Capulus

Capulus, located in the constellation Perseus, is often associated with intense, raw, and assertive energy in astrological interpretations. Representing the handle of Perseus's sword, Capulus is a star of action and determination, characterized by a masculine and dynamic influence. Its energy aligns closely with Mars, embodying themes of courage, aggression, and a drive to overcome obstacles.

Individuals with Capulus prominent in their charts may be drawn to intense experiences, pushing through life's challenges with a bold and sometimes unyielding approach. While this fixed star can bring resilience and focus, it may also lend a rough or confrontational edge if not balanced. Capulus's influence can manifest as a desire to tackle challenges head-on, making it beneficial for those in fields requiring bravery and direct action, such as sports or military pursuits. However, its energy, if unmoderated, may lead to impulsive actions or a tendency toward aggression.

Capulus is often contrasted with its nearby star, Algol, which symbolizes darker themes. In this light, Capulus is seen as a force of vitality and assertive strength, necessary to face adversity. When harmoniously aspected, it grants a strong sense of willpower and courage; when poorly aspected, it may indicate struggles with anger, intensity, or unrefined impulses.

Castor

Located in the constellation Gemini, this star is associated with intellect, creativity, and duality in astrological interpretations. Named after one of the mythical twins Castor and Pollux, Castor represents themes of the mind, communication, and skill. It is thought to influence individuals with a sharp intellect, a talent for learning, and an affinity for creative and intellectual pursuits. Castor's energy can be aligned with Mercury, emphasizing mental agility, language, and adaptability.

Astrologically, Castor's placement is often associated with success in areas requiring communication, writing, and teaching. It tends to bring a versatile nature, making those under its influence adept in multiple fields. However, the duality inherent in the symbol of the twins suggests variability, which can lead to moodiness or shifts in perspective. In its higher expression, Castor represents intellectual achievement and eloquence; however, if negatively aspected, it can manifest as indecision or a propensity for argument.

Some sources note that Castor's influence is also associated with law and justice, as the star encourages the pursuit of truth and balance. While it provides the qualities of a thoughtful leader, it may also bring challenges in maintaining consistency due to its dual nature.

Deneb Adige

The fixed star Deneb Adige (α Cygni), located in the constellation Cygnus, symbolizes creative expression, intellectual pursuits, and the power of eloquence in astrological interpretation. Its name, meaning "tail of the swan," reflects its placement at the end of Cygnus. Deneb Adige is often associated with spiritual wisdom, transformation, and a desire to inspire others.

Astrologically, Deneb Adige's influence is seen as supportive of talents in the arts, literature, and science, encouraging a refined, idealistic, and somewhat mystical character. It is linked with qualities such as charisma, depth of thought, and a natural inclination towards both intellectual and spiritual growth. Individuals influenced by this star may feel drawn to roles where they can enlighten, uplift, or contribute to the cultural or intellectual landscape, particularly through eloquent communication or artistic expression.

Some traditions view Deneb Adige as aligning with the planetary influence of Mercury and Venus, providing a balance of intellect and aesthetics, enhancing social appeal, and fostering artistic talents. This energy can also inspire leadership through creativity, giving those under its influence a unique voice and presence. However, if negatively aspected, Deneb Adige might incline a person toward vanity or the pursuit of fame without substance.

In essence, Deneb Adige represents the swan's grace in blending intellect and artistry, making it an auspicious star for those in creative and intellectual fields, as it fuels inspiration, compassion, and visionary ideas.

Deneb Algedi

Deneb Algedi, a fixed star in the constellation of Capricorn, is traditionally associated with qualities of justice, wisdom, and discipline due to its Saturn-Jupiter nature. In astrological interpretations, it is thought to bring success through ethical actions, lawfulness, and adherence to societal rules. The star is often connected to figures of authority and leadership, especially those who are wise, responsible, and just. When positively aligned, Deneb Algedi can signify high moral standards, honour, and even public or social respect. It has a protective quality, suggesting that those influenced by it can benefit from legal matters or find support in upholding justice.

However, if negatively influenced or poorly aspected in a chart, it may indicate challenges with authority or disputes with regulations. Those under its influence are encouraged to embrace principles of fairness and righteousness to harness its more beneficial attributes. Deneb Algedi is also linked to protection and guidance in financial and legal matters, often suggesting gains when one acts with integrity and responsibility.

Denebola

This is the brightest star in the tail of the constellation Leo. It carries significant astrological meaning with a blend of Mars and Saturn energies. This fixed star is traditionally associated with traits of independence, critical thinking, and a progressive mindset. It often represents a desire to challenge the status quo, promoting innovation and a forward-thinking perspective. Individuals influenced by

Denebola may display a strong sense of personal integrity and a drive to initiate change, sometimes finding themselves in opposition to conventional ideas or authorities.

Astrologically, Denebola is thought to bring sudden and unexpected events, often leading to transformative experiences that encourage personal growth and a new understanding of the world. This star may also be linked to issues of reputation and public perception; its influence can bring notoriety or attention that is not always favourable, especially if individuals act without considering the consequences of their rebellious inclinations. While Denebola can bring both success and controversy, it often rewards those who act with authenticity and maintain their values even in the face of resistance.

When well-aspected, Denebola's energy can manifest as leadership, originality, and clarity in one's life purpose. However, challenging aspects may increase tendencies toward impatience, conflict, and volatility. For best results, those under its influence are encouraged to channel its energy into constructive reform rather than impulsive or reactive behaviour.

Diadem

Diadem, a fixed star in the constellation Coma Berenices, is symbolically linked to sacrifice, devotion, and dedication, particularly in relation to love and loyalty. Named after the diadem or crown of Queen Berenice, this star is often associated with selflessness and commitment, especially within personal relationships or partnerships. It is said to endow those under its influence with qualities of humility, patience, and a tendency to prioritize others' well-being over personal desires.

Diadem suggests an ability to gain recognition and respect through service or sacrifice, often pointing to a quiet strength and resilience. When emphasized in a chart, Diadem can encourage individuals to commit deeply to causes or relationships, showing loyalty even in challenging circumstances. This star's energy is often connected with a protective or nurturing role, symbolizing someone who may choose to support others' achievements rather than seeking the spotlight themselves.

In terms of challenges, Diadem's influence can lead to feelings of being unappreciated or overextended if sacrifices are made without balance. This star encourages self-awareness to ensure that dedication to others does not lead to personal neglect. Positioned well, Diadem can bring fulfillment through service, devotion, and the enduring impact of gentle, supportive influence.

El Nath

El Nath, also known as Beta Tauri, is located at the tip of the northern horn of the constellation Taurus. Astrologically, El Nath combines qualities of Mars and Mercury, symbolizing a strong, assertive energy alongside quick intelligence and communication skills. The star is often associated with martial qualities such as courage, determination, and a readiness to defend or assert oneself, making it an influential point for strength and resilience.

With its Mars-like influence, El Nath encourages individuals to take decisive action, often in defense of personal beliefs or in pursuit of ambitious goals. This star may also bring about challenges that require endurance and bravery, making it significant in charts where overcoming adversity is a theme. Additionally, El Nath is thought to provide the ability to navigate difficult situations with a clear-headed approach, often suggesting a balance between aggression and intellect.

In some interpretations, El Nath represents a penetrating insight and an ability to cut through confusion, especially when well-placed in a natal chart. However, if negatively aspected, it may manifest as impulsiveness or confrontational tendencies. Overall, El Nath supports individuals in harnessing inner strength, assertiveness, and strategic thinking, with an emphasis on protection and standing up for oneself or others.

Facies

Facies, a fixed star in the constellation Sagittarius, is located within the nebula of the Archer's "face." It carries a potent Martian-Plutonic influence, associated with intense, piercing energy and a capacity for resilience in challenging circumstances. In astrology, Facies often represents an unwavering focus, fortitude, and the ability to endure hardship. It is thought to bring determination, insight, and sometimes a sharp intensity to individuals or matters it influences.

However, Facies can also suggest a "tunnel vision" effect, where an intense focus may overshadow other aspects of life, leading to a somewhat uncompromising or even ruthless approach. Due to its Plutonic quality, Facies can represent transformative or cathartic events, often pushing individuals to confront deep-seated issues, particularly in relation to survival instincts, willpower, and perseverance. This influence, while potentially challenging, is frequently associated with profound personal growth and the ability to overcome significant obstacles.

When prominent in a chart, Facies may bring ambition and resilience, but it also warns against extremism or excessive intensity, suggesting a need for balance.

Fomalhaut

Fomalhaut, the brightest star in the constellation Piscis Austrinus, is one of the four Royal Stars of Persia and has a mystical reputation in astrology. Known for its connection to the element of water and symbolizing purity and depth of spirit, Fomalhaut is associated with Neptune's ethereal influence. This star is considered highly auspicious, offering potential for visionary insight, idealism, and artistic or creative expression.

it bestows charisma, allure, and a sense of destiny upon individuals it strongly influences. Its energy is known to inspire profound imagination, spiritual insight, and a drive to pursue higher ideals. However, Fomalhaut also carries a cautionary edge, as it warns against deception, overindulgence, or being misled by illusions. This influence encourages integrity and authenticity to harness the star's positive effects fully.

When well-aspected in a natal chart, Fomalhaut can enhance one's ability to inspire others and manifest creative or spiritual gifts. It's also tied to fame or a legacy, especially in fields that require compassion, empathy, or artistic pursuits. When negatively aspected, however, it may indicate a vulnerability to escapism or disillusionment.

Hamal

Hamal is the brightest star in the constellation Aries. It represents a strong, pioneering spirit and is associated with leadership and assertive energy. It is traditionally linked with Mars and Saturn, giving it a nature that combines strength, determination, and occasionally stubbornness. People with a prominent Hamal in their charts may possess a confident, ambitious nature and a readiness to take charge or break new ground in their endeavours.

Hamal's influence often signifies a desire for independence and self-direction, pushing individuals toward roles where they can lead rather than follow. However, the star's association with Saturn can also bring challenges, such as rigid thinking or difficulties in handling authority. When positively aspected, Hamal can enhance courage, resilience, and the drive to overcome obstacles. In contrast, challenging aspects may bring out tendencies toward confrontation or resistance to change.

Astrologers also note that Hamal symbolizes the beginning of spring in the Northern Hemisphere, aligning it with themes of renewal, growth, and the courage to pursue new ventures. Its influence can foster self-reliance and a pioneering approach to life, making it particularly potent in matters requiring initiative or boldness.

Markab

Markab, located in the constellation Pegasus, is often associated with intellect, honour, and a stable yet somewhat cautious approach to life. Known for its connection to both Mercury and Mars, Markab imparts mental agility, discipline, and strategic thinking, often seen in individuals who excel in fields requiring intellectual rigor or precision, such as science, academia, or military strategy. The star's influence can promote a calm yet assertive demeanour, allowing one to navigate challenges with poise.

Markab's symbolism also reflects themes of fortitude and resilience, particularly in facing difficult situations with a level-headed approach. However, the influence of Mars can occasionally manifest as impatience or a tendency toward restlessness, especially when progress feels stifled. Astrologers advise that Markab's energy be channeled into productive pursuits, as it may otherwise lead to mental strain or overzealousness.

When well-aspected, Markab is believed to bestow honour, recognition, and a solid reputation in one's chosen field. It also encourages the integration of intellect with action, fostering a balance between thought and initiative. On the flip side, challenging aspects can suggest caution against rigid thinking or impulsiveness in decision-making.

Menkar

This fixed star, also known as Alpha Ceti, is located in the constellation Cetus and holds a traditionally challenging astrological influence. Linked with the energy of Saturn, Menkar is associated with themes of fate, collective issues, and the unconscious depths of human experience. It often symbolizes encounters with forces beyond individual control, such as societal or environmental challenges, and suggests lessons around patience and endurance.

Menkar brings awareness to cycles of destruction and renewal, signifying that endings can lead to new beginnings. Individuals with strong Menkar influences in their charts may feel an affinity for collective concerns, environmental issues, or deeply rooted psychological insights. Menkar's energy is often described as one that can prompt individuals to confront fears or hidden aspects of the psyche, sometimes bringing about transformative growth if approached consciously.

While Menkar's Saturnian influence can seem restrictive or challenging, its lessons ultimately encourage resilience and adaptation to the ebb and flow of life's larger cycles. Astrologers recommend working with Menkar's influence to cultivate humility, self-awareness, and acceptance of life's inevitable changes.

Mirach

Mirach (beta Andromedae) is located in the constellation Andromeda. it is associated with harmony, charm, and creativity. Known for its Venusian qualities, Mirach influences areas such as artistic expression, beauty, and nurturing relationships. It is thought to bestow a magnetic and gracious nature, enhancing an individual's sensitivity to beauty, art, and aesthetics. Mirach is also connected with a sense of peace and cooperation, promoting diplomacy and ease in social interactions.

This star supports endeavours that involve kindness, inspiration, and a balanced approach to emotional life. Those with a prominent Mirach influence may find fulfilment through creative pursuits or roles that foster connection and support for others. However, when poorly aspected, it can indicate issues with indecisiveness or over-dependence on external validation.

In horary astrology, Mirach is often seen as a positive influence, symbolizing an environment conducive to peace and well-being. Its energies align well with artistic fields and healing professions, reflecting its association with both beauty and empathy.

Mirfach

The fixed star Mirfach (Mirfak), also known as Alpha Persei, resides in the constellation Perseus. it is noted for its Martian and Jupiterian qualities. Astrologically, Mirfak symbolizes bravery, action, and strength. Those influenced by Mirfak are often seen as resilient and determined, with a natural inclination toward leadership and ambitious pursuits. This star imbues a spirit of courage and adventure, promoting an eagerness to face challenges and take risks.

Mirfak is connected with strength in character and the drive to achieve high aspirations. However, it can also represent the potential for aggressive behaviour or overconfidence if negatively aspected, making balance crucial in harnessing its energy constructively. Mirfak's influence is often favourable in careers or life paths that require assertiveness, quick decision-making, and competitive spirit.

Phact

Phact, also known as Alpha Columbae, is located in the constellation Columba, the Dove. Astrologically, Phact is associated with qualities of journey, exploration, and discovery. It often symbolizes freedom and the desire to break free from restrictions, resonating with themes of peace and safe passage. Phact's influence is generally seen as positive, bringing about a gentle, adventurous spirit and a sense of optimism in facing new ventures.

Those under the influence of Phact may be inclined toward travel or pursuits that foster a sense of peace and harmony.

Phact's energy also encourages a spiritual connection, aligning with the serene and protective symbolism of the dove. However, its influence might sometimes lead to restlessness or a need to roam if not well-directed. Phact's gentle yet exploratory essence is generally well-suited for professions or life paths that involve healing, guidance, and peacemaking.

Pollux

This star, also known as Beta Geminorum (in Gemini), carries a potent and somewhat intense astrological influence, often associated with a Mars-like energy. Known as the "Immortal Twin" alongside Castor, Pollux symbolizes resilience, strength, and a warrior spirit. It can grant bravery, determination, and an assertive edge, enabling individuals to confront challenges with fortitude. In mythology, Pollux is associated with athletic prowess and combat, and this Martian influence suggests a talent for dealing with conflict or adversity effectively.

Pollux is often linked to those who possess courage and the ability to overcome obstacles. However, its influence can also lead to aggressiveness or impulsiveness if not tempered, sometimes manifesting as a "dark" twin aspect.

This star's influence can inspire both physical and intellectual pursuits, driving a passionate, sometimes rebellious nature that seeks justice or independence.

When well-aspected in a natal chart, Pollux can favor success in athletic, military, or competitive fields, with a strong inclination towards leadership. Negatively, it may encourage confrontation or a harsh approach to challenges. Pollux's powerful energy urges one to confront life's battles with both bravery and responsibility, honouring its dual nature.

Procyon

The fixed star Procyon, in the constellation Canis Minor, carries a Mars-Mercury influence, combining swift action with sharp intellect. Its energy is generally favourable, symbolizing success achieved through personal effort, skill, and strategic thinking. Known as a "fortunate" star, Procyon is often associated with resilience and the ability to navigate life's challenges, bringing a quick response to situations and adaptability to changing conditions.

Astrologically, Procyon grants courage, assertiveness, and sometimes a sense of restlessness or urgency. Individuals influenced by Procyon may excel in roles that require rapid decision-making and mental agility, as well as in pursuits that demand physical prowess or endurance. Its Mars influence suggests a readiness to act and a strong drive, while the Mercury aspect brings curiosity and communication skills.

However, Procyon also warns of impulsivity; its influence may lead to hasty decisions or overreactions if not balanced. When favorably aspected, Procyon can bring fame, honour, and swift achievements, but when poorly aspected, it can lead to burnout or challenges from a lack of foresight.

Ras Algethi

Ras Algethi, alpha-Hercules, is found in the constellation Hercules. It holds a Mars-Saturn influence, imbuing it with qualities of strength, endurance, and sometimes intensity or severity. Astrologically, Ras Algethi is known for bestowing a powerful, determined nature, often associated with a strong will and a readiness to tackle life's challenges. It symbolizes inner strength and resilience, offering those it influences the potential for leadership and the ability to overcome adversity through persistence and resolve.

Ras Algethi's Mars-Saturn combination can indicate a no-nonsense approach, valuing discipline, and controlled action. Individuals under its influence may feel compelled to face difficulties head-on, channeling their energy into purposeful endeavours. While the star's energy promotes resilience and resourcefulness, it also warns of a tendency toward rigidity or harshness when overly influenced by Saturn's weight. However, when harmoniously aspected, Ras Algethi's influence can manifest as a balanced power, enabling individuals to take strategic action with patience and persistence, leading to steady success over time.

Ras Alhague

The fixed star Ras Alhague, located in the constellation Ophiuchus, is traditionally associated with the influence of Saturn and Venus. This star often represents the archetype of the healer, mystic, or philosopher. Astrologically, it embodies themes of wisdom, healing, and knowledge, as well as a potential for grappling with dualities, especially in the realms of morality and wellness. People or events influenced by Ras Alhague may find themselves drawn to pursuits in healing, medicine, or philosophy, often embodying a complex understanding of both the material and spiritual aspects of life.

This star can suggest challenges with boundaries, both in a personal and broader sense, and may imply issues related to overindulgence or escapism when poorly aspected. Its Saturnian nature emphasizes responsibility and discipline, while the Venusian influence brings a softer, compassionate aspect, often prompting the drive to help others and a deep involvement in personal or collective healing journeys.

Regulus

Located in the constellation Leo, this is one of the four Royal Stars of Persia, symbolizing leadership, honour, and success. Known as the "Heart of the Lion," Regulus carries a potent influence of Jupiter and Mars, lending it themes of ambition, courage, and authority. Astrologically, Regulus is linked to fame, high status, and the potential for great power or recognition, often rewarding those with a noble character who pursue their goals with integrity.

Regulus is also associated with a need for vigilance against the pitfalls of pride and revenge; misuse of its influence can lead to downfall or public disgrace. When positively aspected, Regulus enhances qualities of generosity, loyalty, and an unwavering commitment to one's vision or cause. Those under Regulus's influence may experience significant success or prominence but are reminded to stay humble and act with kindness to retain their achievements.

Rigel

Rigel, found in the constellation Orion, is associated with success, ambition, and resilience in astrology. It has a Jupiter and Mars influence, which gives it a dynamic, driven energy that can lead to fame and achievements, particularly in areas where courage, skill, and innovation are required. Rigel often signifies success in business, teaching, or leadership roles, encouraging a proactive and assertive approach.

This is seen as a star of opportunities, symbolizing the rewards of hard work and determination. However, its Mars influence also suggests potential challenges or risks that may require resilience and adaptability. This star promotes intelligence, curiosity, and sometimes a teaching or mentoring role for those it influences, as well as a capacity to overcome adversity. With its placement in the foot of Orion, Rigel embodies forward movement and ambition, providing a solid foundation for career accomplishments and personal growth.

Rukbat

Located in the constellation Sagittarius, Rukbat is not as prominent in traditional astrology as some other stars but has unique qualities tied to stability, endurance, and foundation. The name "Rukbat" means "knee" or "leg," as it represents the archer's knee in Sagittarius, symbolizing support, stability, and steady progress.

Rukbat is often associated with a patient and determined nature. It may grant the ability to maintain resilience and perseverance in difficult situations, showing a person's capacity to stand firm and endure. Though it lacks the more dynamic or influential traits of brighter stars, Rukbat is seen as a supportive presence, enhancing reliability and self-discipline. Individuals with strong Rukbat influence may excel in fields requiring a methodical, steady approach rather than sudden actions or changes.

Rukbat's influence suggests a foundational energy that enhances stability, patience, and the quiet strength to stay grounded through challenges. While subtle, it provides essential support to ensure resilience and consistent growth over time.

Sadalmelek

Sadalmelek, found in the constellation Aquarius, is known as "The Lucky Star of the King", as it was associated with the birth of kings. This star traditionally carries themes of fortune, success, and optimistic outcomes, linking it to leadership and beneficial influence. Astrologically, Sadalmelek is said to provide an aura of dignity, honour, and positive recognition, particularly in public or high-profile roles. Its energy aligns with authority and good fortune in career and public reputation.

Sadalmelek's influence can foster personal growth and integrity, particularly where individuals seek to lead or inspire others. Those with strong aspects to Sadalmelek in their natal charts might find support in pursuits involving leadership, teaching, or community work, where their efforts to uplift others bring reciprocal recognition and respect.

Sadalsuud

This star, in the constellation Aquarius is known as "The Luckiest of the Lucky." Astrologically, it has strong connections with good fortune, success, and wisdom, especially when it aligns well with planets in a chart. Sadalsuud is often associated with a generous, humanitarian spirit and a desire to work for the betterment of society, reflecting the Aquarian qualities of community-focused ideals and visionary thinking.

With a Jupiter-like nature, Sadalsuud promotes expansion, positive growth, and beneficial outcomes in endeavours related to leadership, intellectual pursuits, and social causes. Those influenced by Sadalsuud might experience success in public affairs, academic achievements, or roles involving guidance and mentorship. When well-aspected, it can bring high levels of popularity, wealth, and favourable opportunities, whereas challenging aspects may bring the opposite effect, highlighting the need to maintain balance and integrity.

Overall, Sadalsuud is considered one of the more auspicious stars in astrology, promoting uplifting outcomes, especially when tied to altruistic or noble pursuits.

Scheat

Located in the constellation Pegasus, Scheat has a complex astrological reputation. Known for its association with both brilliance and unpredictability, Scheat is often linked with themes of intellect, creativity, and an unconventional outlook, as well as challenges or sudden reversals. Its nature blends influences of Mars and Mercury, which manifest as dynamic mental energy but can also lead to impulsivity and risky behaviour if not well-balanced.

Astrologically, Scheat is connected to both intellectual achievements and potential mishaps, especially involving water or aviation. It can inspire innovative ideas, particularly in areas requiring unique perspectives and analytical skill, but it may also signal a predisposition to issues like accidents, misunderstandings, or strained relationships if negatively aspected. Scheat is known to promote originality and a rebellious spirit, lending individuals a nonconformist outlook that can be beneficial in creative or scientific pursuits. However, caution is advised as it may also amplify tendencies toward emotional or physical turbulence.

In horoscopic terms, those influenced by Scheat are encouraged to ground their creativity and analytical abilities with careful planning and a practical mindset, as its influence can bring both insightful breakthroughs and heightened volatility. Scheat's energy can ultimately foster resilience, pushing one to overcome setbacks and use their intellectual gifts productively.

Schedir

Schedir (Alpha Cassiopeiae) is a fixed star associated with the constellation Cassiopeia and is symbolically tied to themes of strength, dignity, and resilience. Schedir carries the influence of Saturn and Venus, lending it qualities of authority, patience, and a refined sense of beauty. This star is often connected to themes of feminine power, sovereignty, and independence, resonating with the mythological Queen Cassiopeia's pride and regal bearing. Schedir's energy is thought to endow individuals with leadership potential, especially in roles that require grace under pressure and an ability to inspire others. Its influence can enhance qualities like determination and inner strength, especially in situations that involve standing up for one's beliefs or values. However, some traditional interpretations also suggest that Schedir may bring challenges related to arrogance or vanity if poorly aspected, echoing the story of Cassiopeia's downfall due to her hubris.

In a natal chart, Schedir's placement can indicate a dignified, authoritative presence, with a potential for success in leadership, diplomacy, or creative pursuits. However, it is suggested to approach this star's energy with humility to avoid the pitfalls of excessive pride or obstinacy. Overall, Schedir offers a powerful mix of Saturnian discipline and Venusian grace, making it a star of regal resilience and inner fortitude.

Sirius

Sirius, known as the Dog Star and located in the constellation Canis Major, is one of the most significant fixed stars in astrology due to its brightness and mythological background. Astrologically, Sirius is associated with success, fame, and honour, largely due to its connection with Jupiter and Mars energies. The star is thought to amplify personal ambition, leadership potential, and achievements, often bringing a high status or recognition to those with prominent Sirius placements in their natal charts.

Ancient astrologers saw Sirius as a protector, symbolizing power and guardianship. It has been associated with qualities like resilience, loyalty, and tenacity. Sirius's influence is also linked with passionate pursuits, encouraging individuals to pursue their goals with vigour and enthusiasm. Additionally, in some interpretations, Sirius connects to spiritual insight, symbolizing a bridge between the earthly and the divine realms.

In its potentially challenging aspect, Sirius can push individuals toward extremes, fostering an intense drive that, without balance, might lead to burnout or excessive pride. Its influence is most positively expressed through disciplined actions and maintaining humility, using its energy for the greater good.

Spica

Spica, located in the constellation Virgo, is one of the most auspicious fixed stars in astrology. Known as a star of protection and fortune, Spica is strongly linked to Venus and Mars energies, symbolizing both beauty and strength. Astrologically, it is associated with success, creativity, and achievement, often marking individuals with natural talents in the arts, sciences, and intellectual pursuits. People with a prominent Spica placement in their charts may experience fame, recognition, and financial gain, as Spica is seen as a harbinger of prosperity.

Spica is also considered a marker of spiritual protection and insight. In many interpretations, it signifies divine gifts and blessings, enhancing qualities of generosity and kindness. This star's influence fosters optimism, honour, and the potential to excel in academic and philosophical realms. However, while generally positive, its influence can incline individuals toward perfectionism or intense self-criticism if its energy is not channeled productively.

With its nurturing and protective qualities, Spica is often seen as a beneficial force, providing guidance and stability, particularly in times of uncertainty. This star is thought to support those who align with their higher purpose and work for the betterment of others, amplifying positive traits and rewarding effort with success and fulfilment.

Sualocin

The fixed star Sualocin is found in the constellation Delphinus. It carries associations of playfulness, creativity, and strategic intelligence due to its position in a dolphin-shaped constellation. It embodies qualities of wit, curiosity, and an affinity for artistic or intellectual pursuits. Those with Sualocin prominent in their chart might exhibit quick-thinking, adaptability, and a certain charisma that draws others toward them. This star also symbolizes resourcefulness, often marking individuals with a knack for problem-solving or unique forms of self-expression.

In some esoteric interpretations, Sualocin's energy resonates with that of Neptune, lending individuals with this influence a spiritual or mystical inclination, which may manifest as an interest in the metaphysical or in imaginative activities such as writing, music, or performance. Sualocin's influence can bring positive opportunities in these areas, encouraging personal growth and sometimes fame for those in creative fields.

However, the star's light-hearted energy can sometimes lead to a tendency to evade serious responsibilities if not balanced, favouring a need for constant stimulation. For those looking to harness its energy, Sualocin supports mental agility, intuition, and the ability to navigate life with adaptability and charm.

Toliman

Also known as Alpha Centauri, Toliman is significant in astrology for its associations with learning, guidance, and wisdom. Traditionally considered to have a Venus-Jupiter influence, Toliman imparts a generally positive energy, emphasizing qualities like harmony, kindness, and strong ethical principles. It often grants individuals a natural inclination toward teaching, counselling, or mentoring roles, where they can provide support and insight to others. Toliman may enhance intellectual curiosity and the desire for growth and self-improvement. It encourages a balanced, thoughtful approach to life, favouring relationships that are grounded in mutual respect and understanding. Those with Toliman prominent in their chart might experience beneficial opportunities, especially in areas related to education, social service, or creative expression. However, there can be a tendency toward idealism or being overly accommodating, which may need balancing with practical perspectives.

Toliman's Venus-Jupiter nature suggests that its influence often brings prosperity and warmth, emphasizing generosity and the importance of moral values. The star supports those who seek to connect deeply with others, particularly through shared knowledge or a commitment to higher principles.

Vega

This star in the constellation Lyra is renowned in astrology for its strong, charismatic, and influential nature. Known for its connection to artistic expression, music, and eloquence, Vega has a Venus-Mercury influence, bringing qualities of beauty, charm, and intellectual agility. This star is often associated with success in the arts, diplomacy, and communication, highlighting the capacity to captivate and inspire others.

Vega's energy can also manifest as an attraction to fame and recognition, and it often enhances one's public image and appeal. However, its influence may come with a need to balance idealism with humility, as it can foster intense ambition and, at times, a desire for prominence that may lead to arrogance. In horoscopes, Vega is thought to bestow wisdom, a philosophical nature, and an appreciation for the finer things in life.

When well-aspected, Vega supports constructive use of one's talents, ethical pursuits, and a harmonious influence. If poorly aspected, it may incline toward excessive pride, indulgence, or misplaced values. Astrologers often view Vega's placement as a marker for those destined to leave a legacy, especially in areas that involve speaking, writing, or performance. Its placement in a chart can indicate a powerful and positive influence in professional success and personal charisma.

Vindemiatrix

Vindemiatrix (epsilon Virginis) is located in the right arm of the maiden, Virgo. It is often associated with a Saturn-Mercury influence in astrology, lending a sense of gravity, critical thinking, and practicality. This star, also known as the "Grape Gatherer," historically connects to themes of harvest, loss, and maturity. Astrologically, Vindemiatrix is believed to signify experiences that foster wisdom through hardship or introspection.

People influenced by Vindemiatrix are often seen as insightful and perceptive, yet may experience challenges related to loss, responsibility, or duty, which lead to growth and understanding. Vindemiatrix's influence is known for encouraging intellectual and analytical pursuits, often prompting interest in writing, research, or communication fields, as it enhances a person's capacity to observe and evaluate details critically.

However, Vindemiatrix also has a challenging aspect, as it may bring inclinations toward pessimism, rigidity, or melancholic tendencies. It suggests that lessons of resilience and perseverance are central themes, encouraging individuals to find strength in adversity. When well-aspected in a chart, Vindemiatrix can support thoughtful insight and responsible leadership, whereas a challenging placement may highlight struggles with grief or a tendency toward overly analytical or skeptical mindsets.

Zosma

Zosma, a fixed star in the constellation Leo, is often associated with qualities of self-sacrifice, sensitivity, and, at times, victimization or loss. it has a Saturn-Venus influence, which brings both creative and melancholic elements, making it a star of empathy, caution, and awareness. Individuals strongly connected to Zosma may feel a heightened sense of responsibility to help others, often at their own expense, leading to themes of service, martyrdom, or compassion.

It can signal a tendency toward introspection and can heighten intuition or psychic abilities. However, it also brings awareness of suffering or hardships, suggesting that those influenced by it may encounter life challenges that ultimately foster personal growth, empathy, and resilience. This star encourages an understanding of boundaries to avoid excessive self-sacrifice and highlights the importance of channelling empathetic insights constructively.

When positively aspected in a chart, Zosma can enhance compassion, creativity, and a drive to support others in a balanced way. Negatively aspected, it may point to struggles with victim mentality or feelings of depletion due to overextension in service to others. In summary, Zosma brings lessons of balance, resilience, and the careful navigation between empathy and self-preservation.

Zuben Elgenubi

Located in the constellation Libra, Zuben Elgenubi carries a Saturn-Venus influence, often connecting to themes of justice, balance, and ethical dilemmas. This fixed star is thought to highlight the individual's moral and social responsibilities and may signal a focus on fairness, partnerships, and humanitarian efforts. Astrologically, Zuben Elgenubi encourages discernment, especially in social relationships, and can denote an inclination toward supporting social or collective causes.

When prominent in a chart, Zuben Elgenubi can represent a tendency to confront or resolve imbalances in society, sometimes through personal challenges that teach lessons about integrity and justice. Positive aspects to Zuben Elgenubi can enhance the ability to achieve harmony in relationships and support fair dealings, while difficult aspects may bring challenges around ethical decision-making or social sacrifice. The star's energy encourages navigating the balance between self-interest and the collective good, often helping the individual develop wisdom and a stronger moral compass.

Zuben Eschamali

Zuben Eschamali (beta Librae) is found in the constellation Libra. It is often associated with Jupiter and Mercury, bringing themes of justice, balance, and wisdom. It is regarded as a star that influences integrity, ethics, and truth-seeking, emphasizing intellectual pursuits and an inclination toward fairness. Traditionally, Zuben Eschamali is seen as a star that can signify success, particularly in areas involving communication, diplomacy, and law.

When well-aspected, Zuben Eschamali promotes harmony, ambition in social justice, and can confer leadership in legal or moral endeavours. It supports those with a clear sense of purpose and a dedication to higher principles. If negatively aspected, the star's influence may bring struggles in maintaining objectivity or dealing with issues around fairness and responsibility.

Zuben Eschamali, therefore, guides individuals toward achieving justice and contributes to a balanced worldview, making it especially relevant in charts that emphasize mediation, negotiation, or humanitarian causes.

PLANETS WITH THE FIXED STARS IN 2025

It is obvious from the following tables that the fast moving bodies will have more frequent conjunctions with the fixed stars than the slow outer planets. For example, the Moon will have recurrent contacts with the same stars on a monthly basis, whereas in the case of Pluto it could take several hundred years.

What follows is a summary of the main conjunctions of the slow-moving planets and the North Node with the fixed stars. The ecliptic longitudes are given within the tropical zodiac.

Pluto will be between 1°04' and 3°49' Aquarius throughout 2025. It will be conjunct Altair on August 14th and December 11th. In the past it has been linked with epic battles bringing about long lasting geopolitical changes. I have discussed this conjunction in greater detail on my blog at codexcelestial.com.

Neptune in 2025 will be located between 28°18' Pisces and 2°10' Aries. It will be conjunct Scheat on March 22nd and

November 4th. According to Ptolemy this fixed star is of the nature of Mars and Mercury; to other authors, of Saturn and Mercury; It causes extreme misfortune, murder, suicide, and drowning. Scheat is an especially unfortunate star regarding the sea. It was said to indicate danger from that element in the form of tidal waves or violent storms.

Uranus in 2025 will be found between 23°16' Taurus and 1°28' Gemini. It will conjunct Capulus on March 26th, Algol on April 18th and Alcyone on June 26th and November 20th. All of these stars have negative connotations, being associated with violence, physical harms, and mass casualties.

Saturn in 2025 will be between 14°31' Pisces and 1°56' Aries. It will conjunct Markab on March 19th, and Scheat on May 21st and September 5th. Markab, or alpha-Pegasi, traditionally can have mixed effects, including honour and riches but also danger of wounds, fire and sudden death.

Jupiter in 2025 will be found between 11°17' Gemini and 25°9' of Cancer. From early April until the end of the year it will conjunct 13 fixed stars, including Betelgeuse on June

2nd and Sirius on August 9th. Both of these major stars can have mixed effects.

Chiron in 2025 will be located between 19°00' and 27°10' of Aries. There are no major stars in this section of the zodiac.

The North Lunar Node (mean value) will move between 1°30' Aries and 12°13' Pisces. It will conjunct Scheat on January 13th, Markab on June 11th, Ankaa (theta-Aquarii) on November 18th and Achernar on November 19th. This author could not find any literature on the effects of nodal conjunctions with the fixed stars. This is an area that warrants further research.

BRADY'S 60 FIXED STARS:
ALPHABETICAL ORDER

* Achernar   - Constellation: Eridanus, Tropical Longitude: 15°38' Pisces, Sidereal Longitude: 21°27' Aquarius, Declination: -57°07'

* Acrux   - Constellation: Crux, Tropical Longitude: 12°11' Scorpio, Sidereal Longitude: 18°00' Libra, Declination: -63°13'

* Acubens   - Constellation: Cancer, Tropical Longitude: 13°58' Leo, Sidereal Longitude: 19°47' Cancer, Declination: 11°45'

* Aculeus   - Constellation: Scorpio, Tropical Longitude: 26°07' Sagittarius, Sidereal Longitude: 1°55' Sagittarius, Declination: -32°15'

* Acumen   - Constellation: Scorpio, Tropical Longitude: 29°02' Sagittarius, Sidereal Longitude: 4°50' Sagittarius, Declination: -34°47'

* Agena   - Constellation: Centaurus, Tropical Longitude: 24°07' Scorpio, Sidereal Longitude: 29°55' Libra, Declination: -60°29'

* Alcyone   - Constellation: Taurus, Tropical Longitude: 0°19' Gemini, Sidereal Longitude: 6°08' Taurus, Declination: 24°10'

* Aldebaran   - Constellation: Taurus, Tropical Longitude: 10°07' Gemini, Sidereal Longitude: 15°56' Taurus, Declination: 16°33'

* Algol - Constellation: Perseus, Tropical Longitude:
26°30' Taurus, Sidereal Longitude: 2°18' Taurus,
Declination: 41°03'

* Alhena - Constellation: Gemini, Tropical Longitude:
9°26' Cancer, Sidereal Longitude: 15°15' Gemini,
Declination: 16°22'

* Alkes - Constellation: Crater, Tropical Longitude:
24°01' Virgo, Sidereal Longitude: 29°49' Leo, Declination:
-18°25'

* Alnilam - Constellation: Orion, Tropical Longitude:
23°48' Gemini, Sidereal Longitude: 29°36' Taurus,
Declination: -1°11'

* Alphard - Constellation: Hydra, Tropical Longitude:
27°36' Leo, Sidereal Longitude: 3°25' Leo, Declination: -
8°45'

* Alphecca - Constellation: Corona Borealis, Tropical
Longitude: 12°37' Scorpio, Sidereal Longitude: 18°26'
Libra, Declination: 26°37'

* Alpheraz - Constellation: Andromeda, Tropical
Longitude: 14°38' Aries, Sidereal Longitude: 20°27' Pisces,
Declination: 29°13'

* Al Rischa - Constellation: Pisces, Tropical Longitude:
29°42' Aries, Sidereal Longitude: 5°31' Aries, Declination:
2°52'

* Altair - Constellation: Aquila, Tropical Longitude: 2°06'
Aquarius, Sidereal Longitude: 7°55' Capricorn,
Declination: 8°55'

* Ankaa - Constellation: Phoenix, Tropical Longitude: 15°49' Pisces, Sidereal Longitude: 21°38' Aquarius, Declination: -42°10'

* Antares - Constellation: Scorpio, Tropical Longitude: 10°05' Sagittarius, Sidereal Longitude: 15°54' Scorpio, Declination: -26°29'

* Arcturus - Constellation: Bootes, Tropical Longitude: 24°33' Libra, Sidereal Longitude: 0°22' Libra, Declination: 19°03'

* Bellatrix - Constellation: Orion, Tropical Longitude: 21°17' Gemini, Sidereal Longitude: 27°05' Taurus, Declination: 6°22'

* Betelgeuse - Constellation: Orion, Tropical Longitude: 29°05' Gemini, Sidereal Longitude: 4°54' Gemini, Declination: 7°24'

* Canopus - Constellation: Carina, Tropical Longitude: 15°18' Cancer, Sidereal Longitude: 21°07' Gemini, Declination: -52°42'

* Capella - Constellation: Auriga, Tropical Longitude: 22°11' Gemini, Sidereal Longitude: 28°00' Taurus, Declination: 46°01'

* Capulus - Constellation: Perseus, Tropical Longitude: 24°31' Taurus, Sidereal Longitude: 0°19' Taurus, Declination: 57°14'

* Castor - Constellation: Gemini, Tropical Longitude: 20°34' Cancer, Sidereal Longitude: 26°23' Gemini, Declination: 31°50'

* Deneb Adige   - Constellation: Cygnus, Tropical Longitude: 5°39' Pisces, Sidereal Longitude: 11°27' Aquarius, Declination: 45°22'

* Deneb Algedi   - Constellation: Capricorn, Tropical Longitude: 23°52' Aquarius, Sidereal Longitude: 29°40' Capricorn, Declination: -16°01'

* Denebola   - Constellation: Leo, Tropical Longitude: 21°57' Virgo, Sidereal Longitude: 27°45' Leo, Declination: 14°26'

* Diadem   - Constellation: Coma Berenices, Tropical Longitude: 9°16' Libra, Sidereal Longitude: 15°05' Virgo, Declination: 17°24'

* El Nath   - Constellation: Taurus, Tropical Longitude: 22°54' Gemini, Sidereal Longitude: 28°43' Taurus, Declination: 28°37'

* Facies   - Constellation: Sagittarius, Tropical Longitude: 8°38' Capricorn, Sidereal Longitude: 14°27' Sagittarius, Declination: -23°53'

* Fomalhaut   - Constellation: Piscis Austrinus, Tropical Longitude: 4°11' Pisces, Sidereal Longitude: 10°00' Aquarius, Declination: -29°29'

* Hamal   - Constellation: Aries, Tropical Longitude: 7°59' Taurus, Sidereal Longitude: 13°48' Aries, Declination: 23°34'

* Markab   - Constellation: Pegasus, Tropical Longitude: 23°49' Pisces, Sidereal Longitude: 29°37' Aquarius, Declination: 15°20'

* Menkar   - Constellation: Cetus, Tropical Longitude: 14°39' Taurus, Sidereal Longitude: 20°28' Aries, Declination: 4°11'

* Mirach   - Constellation: Andromeda, Tropical Longitude: 0°44' Taurus, Sidereal Longitude: 6°33' Aries, Declination: 35°45'

* Mirfach   - Constellation: Perseus, Tropical Longitude: 2°25' Gemini, Sidereal Longitude: 8°13' Taurus, Declination: 49°56'
* Mirzam (Al Murzims)   - Constellation: Canis Major, Tropical Longitude: 7°31' Cancer, Sidereal Longitude: 13°20' Gemini, Declination: -17°58'

* Phact   - Constellation: Columba, Tropical Longitude: 22°30' Gemini, Sidereal Longitude: 28°19' Taurus, Declination: -34°03'

* Pollux   - Constellation: Gemini, Tropical Longitude: 23°33' Cancer, Sidereal Longitude: 29°21' Gemini, Declination: 27°58'

* Procyon   - Constellation: Canis Minor, Tropical Longitude: 26°07' Cancer, Sidereal Longitude: 1°55' Cancer, Declination: 5°09'

* Ras Algethi   - Constellation: Hercules, Tropical Longitude: 16°28' Sagittarius, Sidereal Longitude: 22°17' Scorpio, Declination: 14°21'

* Ras Alhague   - Constellation: Ophiuchus, Tropical Longitude: 22°46' Sagittarius, Sidereal Longitude: 28°35' Scorpio, Declination: 12°32'

* Regulus   - Constellation: Leo, Tropical Longitude: 0°09' Virgo, Sidereal Longitude: 5°58' Leo, Declination: 11°50'

* Rigel   - Constellation: Orion, Tropical Longitude: 17°10' Gemini, Sidereal Longitude: 22°58 Taurus, Declination: -8°10'

* Rukbat   - Constellation: Sagittarius, Tropical Longitude: 16°57' Capricorn, Sidereal Longitude: 22°46' Sagittarius, Declination: -40°34'

* Sadalmelek   - Constellation: Aquarius, Tropical Longitude: 3°40' Pisces, Sidereal Longitude: 9°29' Aquarius, Declination: -0°12'

* Sadalsuud   - Constellation: Aquarius, Tropical Longitude: 23°43' Aquarius, Sidereal Longitude: 29°32' Capricorn, Declination: -5°28'

* Scheat   - Constellation: Pegasus, Tropical Longitude: 29°42' Pisces, Sidereal Longitude: 5°30' Pisces, Declination: 28°12'

* Schedir (Schedar)   - Constellation: Cassiopeia, Tropical Longitude: 8°07' Taurus, Sidereal Longitude: 13°55' Aries, Declination: 56°40'

* Sirius   - Constellation: Canis Major, Tropical Longitude: 14°25' Cancer, Sidereal Longitude: 20°13' Gemini, Declination: -16°44'

* Spica   - Constellation: Virgo, Tropical Longitude: 24°10' Libra, Sidereal Longitude: 29°58' Virgo, Declination: -11°17'

* Sualocin   - Constellation: Delphinus, Tropical
Longitude: 17°42' Aquarius, Sidereal Longitude: 23°31'
Capricorn, Declination: 15°59'

* Toliman   - Constellation: Centaurus, Tropical Longitude:
29°46' Scorpio, Sidereal Longitude: 5°35' Scorpio,
Declination: -60°55'

* Vega   - Constellation: Lyra, Tropical Longitude: 15°38'
Capricorn, Sidereal Longitude: 21°26' Sagittarius,
Declination: 38°48'

* Vindemiatrix   - Constellation: Virgo, Tropical Longitude:
10°16' Libra, Sidereal Longitude: 16°04' Virgo,
Declination: 10°49'

* Zosma   - Constellation: Leo, Tropical Longitude: 11°39'
Virgo, Sidereal Longitude: 17°27' Leo, Declination: 20°23'

* Zuben Elgenubi   - Constellation: Libra, Tropical
Longitude: 15°24'
Scorpio, Sidereal Longitude: 21°13' Libra, Declination: -
16°08'

* Zuben Eschamali   - Constellation: Libra, Tropical
Longitude: 19°42' Scorpio, Sidereal Longitude: 25°30'
Libra, Declination: -9°28'

BRADY'S 60 FIXED STARS:
ZODIAC ORDER

* Alpheraz   - Constellation: Andromeda, Tropical Longitude: 14°38' Aries, Sidereal Longitude: 20°27' Pisces, Declination: 29°13'

* Al Rischa   - Constellation: Pisces, Tropical Longitude: 29°42' Aries, Sidereal Longitude: 5°31' Aries, Declination: 2°52'

* Mirach   - Constellation: Andromeda, Tropical Longitude: 0°44' Taurus, Sidereal Longitude: 6°33' Aries, Declination: 35°45'

* Hamal   - Constellation: Aries, Tropical Longitude: 7°59' Taurus, Sidereal Longitude: 13°48' Aries, Declination: 23°34'

* Schedir (Schedar)   - Constellation: Cassiopeia, Tropical Longitude: 8°07' Taurus, Sidereal Longitude: 13°55' Aries, Declination: 56°40'

* Menkar   - Constellation: Cetus, Tropical Longitude: 14°39' Taurus, Sidereal Longitude: 20°28' Aries, Declination: 4°11'

* Capulus   - Constellation: Perseus, Tropical Longitude: 24°31' Taurus, Sidereal Longitude: 0°19' Taurus, Declination: 57°14'

* Algol   - Constellation: Perseus, Tropical Longitude: 26°30' Taurus, Sidereal Longitude: 2°18' Taurus, Declination: 41°03'

* Alcyone   - Constellation: Taurus, Tropical Longitude:
0°19' Gemini, Sidereal Longitude: 6°08' Taurus,
Declination: 24°10'

* Mirfach   - Constellation: Perseus, Tropical Longitude:
2°25' Gemini, Sidereal Longitude: 8°13' Taurus,
Declination: 49°56'

* Aldebaran   - Constellation: Taurus, Tropical Longitude:
10°07' Gemini, Sidereal Longitude: 15°56' Taurus,
Declination: 16°33'

* Rigel   - Constellation: Orion, Tropical Longitude: 17°10'
Gemini, Sidereal Longitude: 22°58' Taurus, Declination: -
8°10'

* Bellatrix   - Constellation: Orion, Tropical Longitude:
21°17' Gemini, Sidereal Longitude: 27°05' Taurus,
Declination: 6°22'

* Capella   - Constellation: Auriga, Tropical Longitude:
22°11' Gemini, Sidereal Longitude: 28°00' Taurus,
Declination: 46°01'

* Phact   - Constellation: Columba, Tropical Longitude:
22°30' Gemini, Sidereal Longitude: 28°19' Taurus,
Declination: -34°03'

* El Nath   - Constellation: Taurus, Tropical Longitude:
22°54' Gemini, Sidereal Longitude: 28°43' Taurus,
Declination: 28°37'

* Alnilam   - Constellation: Orion, Tropical Longitude:
23°48' Gemini, Sidereal Longitude: 29°36' Taurus,
Declination: -1°11'

* Betelgeuse   - Constellation: Orion, Tropical Longitude:
29°05' Gemini, Sidereal Longitude: 4°54' Gemini,
Declination: 7°24'

* Mirzam (Al Murzims)   - Constellation: Canis Major,
Tropical Longitude: 7°31' Cancer, Sidereal Longitude:
13°20' Gemini, Declination: -17°58'

* Alhena   - Constellation: Gemini, Tropical Longitude:
9°26' Cancer, Sidereal Longitude: 15°15' Gemini,
Declination: 16°22'

* Sirius   - Constellation: Canis Major, Tropical Longitude:
14°25' Cancer, Sidereal Longitude: 20°13' Gemini,
Declination: -16°44'

* Canopus   - Constellation: Carina, Tropical Longitude:
15°18' Cancer, Sidereal Longitude: 21°07' Gemini,
Declination: -52°42'

* Castor   - Constellation: Gemini, Tropical Longitude:
20°34' Cancer, Sidereal Longitude: 26°23' Gemini,
Declination: 31°50'

* Pollux   - Constellation: Gemini, Tropical Longitude:
23°33' Cancer, Sidereal Longitude: 29°21' Gemini,
Declination: 27°58'

* Procyon   - Constellation: Canis Minor, Tropical
Longitude: 26°07' Cancer, Sidereal Longitude: 1°55'
Cancer, Declination: 5°09'

* Acubens   - Constellation: Cancer, Tropical Longitude:
13°58' Leo, Sidereal Longitude: 19°47' Cancer,
Declination: 11°45'

* Alphard   - Constellation: Hydra, Tropical Longitude:
27°36' Leo, Sidereal Longitude: 3°25' Leo, Declination: -
8°45'

* Regulus   - Constellation: Leo, Tropical Longitude: 0°09'
Virgo, Sidereal Longitude: 5°58' Leo, Declination: 11°50'

* Zosma   - Constellation: Leo, Tropical Longitude: 11°39'
Virgo, Sidereal Longitude: 17°27' Leo, Declination: 20°23'

* Denebola   - Constellation: Leo, Tropical Longitude:
21°57' Virgo, Sidereal Longitude: 27°45' Leo, Declination:
14°26'

* Alkes   - Constellation: Crater, Tropical Longitude:
24°01' Virgo, Sidereal Longitude: 29°49' Leo, Declination:
-18°25'

* Diadem   - Constellation: Coma Berenices, Tropical
Longitude: 9°16' Libra, Sidereal Longitude: 15°05' Virgo,
Declination: 17°24'

* Vindemiatrix   - Constellation: Virgo, Tropical Longitude:
10°16' Libra, Sidereal Longitude: 16°04' Virgo,
Declination: 10°49'

* Spica   - Constellation: Virgo, Tropical Longitude: 24°10'
Libra, Sidereal Longitude: 29°58' Virgo, Declination: -
11°17'

* Arcturus   - Constellation: Bootes, Tropical Longitude:
24°33' Libra, Sidereal Longitude: 0°22' Libra, Declination:
19°03'

* Acrux   - Constellation: Crux, Tropical Longitude: 12°11' Scorpio, Sidereal Longitude: 18°00' Libra, Declination: -63°13'

* Alphecca   - Constellation: Corona Borealis, Tropical Longitude: 12°37' Scorpio, Sidereal Longitude: 18°26' Libra, Declination: 26°37'

* Zuben Elgenubi   - Constellation: Libra, Tropical Longitude: 15°24' Scorpio, Sidereal Longitude: 21°13' Libra, Declination: -16°08'

* Zuben Eschamali   - Constellation: Libra, Tropical Longitude: 19°42' Scorpio, Sidereal Longitude: 25°30' Libra, Declination: -9°28'

* Agena   - Constellation: Centaurus, Tropical Longitude: 24°07' Scorpio, Sidereal Longitude: 29°55' Libra, Declination: -60°29'

* Toliman   - Constellation: Centaurus, Tropical Longitude: 29°46' Scorpio, Sidereal Longitude: 5°35' Scorpio, Declination: -60°55'

* Antares   - Constellation: Scorpio, Tropical Longitude: 10°05' Sagittarius, Sidereal Longitude: 15°54' Scorpio, Declination: -26°29'

* Ras Algethi   - Constellation: Hercules, Tropical Longitude: 16°28' Sagittarius, Sidereal Longitude: 22°17' Scorpio, Declination: 14°21'

* Ras Alhague   - Constellation: Ophiuchus, Tropical Longitude: 22°46' Sagittarius, Sidereal Longitude: 28°35' Scorpio, Declination: 12°32'

* Aculeus   - Constellation: Scorpio, Tropical Longitude:
26°07' Sagittarius, Sidereal Longitude: 1°55' Sagittarius,
Declination: -32°15'

* Acumen   - Constellation: Scorpio, Tropical Longitude:
29°02' Sagittarius, Sidereal Longitude: 4°50' Sagittarius,
Declination: -34°47'

* Facies   - Constellation: Sagittarius, Tropical Longitude:
8°38' Capricorn, Sidereal Longitude: 14°27' Sagittarius,
Declination: -23°53'

* Vega   - Constellation: Lyra, Tropical Longitude: 15°38'
Capricorn, Sidereal Longitude: 21°26' Sagittarius,
Declination: 38°48'

* Rukbat   - Constellation: Sagittarius, Tropical Longitude:
16°57' Capricorn, Sidereal Longitude: 22°46' Sagittarius,
Declination: -40°34'

* Altair   - Constellation: Aquila, Tropical Longitude: 2°06'
Aquarius, Sidereal Longitude: 7°55' Capricorn,
Declination: 8°55'

* Sualocin   - Constellation: Delphinus, Tropical
Longitude: 17°42' Aquarius, Sidereal Longitude: 23°31'
Capricorn, Declination: 15°59'

* Sadalsuud   - Constellation: Aquarius, Tropical
Longitude: 23°43' Aquarius, Sidereal Longitude: 29°32'
Capricorn, Declination: -5°28'

* Deneb Algedi   - Constellation: Capricorn, Tropical
Longitude: 23°52' Aquarius, Sidereal Longitude: 29°40'
Capricorn, Declination: -16°01'

* Sadalmelek   - Constellation: Aquarius, Tropical Longitude: 3°40' Pisces, Sidereal Longitude: 9°29' Aquarius, Declination: -0°12'

* Fomalhaut   - Constellation: Piscis Austrinus, Tropical Longitude: 4°11' Pisces, Sidereal Longitude: 10°00' Aquarius, Declination: -29°29'

* Deneb Adige   - Constellation: Cygnus, Tropical Longitude: 5°39' Pisces, Sidereal Longitude: 11°27' Aquarius, Declination: 45°22'

* Achernar   - Constellation: Eridanus, Tropical Longitude: 15°38' Pisces, Sidereal Longitude: 21°27' Aquarius, Declination: -57°07'

* Ankaa   - Constellation: Phoenix, Tropical Longitude: 15°49' Pisces, Sidereal Longitude: 21°38' Aquarius, Declination: -42°10'

* Markab   - Constellation: Pegasus, Tropical Longitude: 23°49' Pisces, Sidereal Longitude: 29°37' Aquarius, Declination: 15°20'

* Scheat   - Constellation: Pegasus, Tropical Longitude: 29°42' Pisces, Sidereal Longitude: 5°30' Pisces, Declination: 28°12'

BRADY'S 60 FIXED STARS:
DESCENDING DECLINATION ORDER

* Capulus - Constellation: Perseus, Tropical Longitude:
24°31' Taurus, Sidereal Longitude: 0°19' Taurus,
Declination: 57°14'

* Schedir (Schedar) - Constellation: Cassiopeia, Tropical
Longitude: 8°07' Taurus, Sidereal Longitude: 13°55' Aries,
Declination: 56°40'

* Mirfach - Constellation: Perseus, Tropical Longitude:
2°25' Gemini, Sidereal Longitude: 8°13' Taurus,
Declination: 49°56'

* Capella - Constellation: Auriga, Tropical Longitude:
22°11' Gemini, Sidereal Longitude: 28°00' Taurus,
Declination: 46°01'

* Deneb Adige - Constellation: Cygnus, Tropical
Longitude: 5°39' Pisces, Sidereal Longitude: 11°27'
Aquarius, Declination: 45°22'

* Algol - Constellation: Perseus, Tropical Longitude:
26°30' Taurus, Sidereal Longitude: 2°18' Taurus,
Declination: 41°03'

* Vega - Constellation: Lyra, Tropical Longitude: 15°38'
Capricorn, Sidereal Longitude: 21°26' Sagittarius,
Declination: 38°48'

* Mirach - Constellation: Andromeda, Tropical Longitude:
0°44' Taurus, Sidereal Longitude: 6°33' Aries, Declination:
35°45'

* Castor   - Constellation: Gemini, Tropical Longitude:
20°34' Cancer, Sidereal Longitude: 26°23' Gemini,
Declination: 31°50'

* Alpheraz   - Constellation: Andromeda, Tropical
Longitude: 14°38' Aries, Sidereal Longitude: 20°27' Pisces,
Declination: 29°13'

* El Nath   - Constellation: Taurus, Tropical Longitude:
22°54' Gemini, Sidereal Longitude: 28°43' Taurus,
Declination: 28°37'

* Scheat   - Constellation: Pegasus, Tropical Longitude:
29°42' Pisces, Sidereal Longitude: 5°30' Pisces,
Declination: 28°12'

* Pollux   - Constellation: Gemini, Tropical Longitude:
23°33' Cancer, Sidereal Longitude: 29°21' Gemini,
Declination: 27°58'

* Alphecca   - Constellation: Corona Borealis, Tropical
Longitude: 12°37' Scorpio, Sidereal Longitude: 18°26'
Libra, Declination: 26°37'

* Alcyone   - Constellation: Taurus, Tropical Longitude:
0°19' Gemini, Sidereal Longitude: 6°08' Taurus,
Declination: 24°10'

* Hamal   - Constellation: Aries, Tropical Longitude: 7°59'
Taurus, Sidereal Longitude: 13°48' Aries, Declination:
23°34'

* Zosma   - Constellation: Leo, Tropical Longitude: 11°39'
Virgo, Sidereal Longitude: 17°27' Leo, Declination: 20°23'

* Arcturus   - Constellation: Bootes, Tropical Longitude: 24°33' Libra, Sidereal Longitude: 0°22' Libra, Declination: 19°03'

* Diadem   - Constellation: Coma Berenices, Tropical Longitude: 9°16' Libra, Sidereal Longitude: 15°05' Virgo, Declination: 17°24'

* Aldebaran   - Constellation: Taurus, Tropical Longitude: 10°07' Gemini, Sidereal Longitude: 15°56' Taurus, Declination: 16°33'

* Alhena   - Constellation: Gemini, Tropical Longitude: 9°26' Cancer, Sidereal Longitude: 15°15' Gemini, Declination: 16°22'

* Sualocin   - Constellation: Delphinus, Tropical Longitude: 17°42' Aquarius, Sidereal Longitude: 23°31' Capricorn, Declination: 15°59'

* Markab   - Constellation: Pegasus, Tropical Longitude: 23°49' Pisces, Sidereal Longitude: 29°37' Aquarius, Declination: 15°20'

* Denebola   - Constellation: Leo, Tropical Longitude: 21°57' Virgo, Sidereal Longitude: 27°45' Leo, Declination: 14°26'

* Ras Algethi   - Constellation: Hercules, Tropical Longitude: 16°28' Sagittarius, Sidereal Longitude: 22°17' Scorpio, Declination: 14°21'

* Ras Alhague   - Constellation: Ophiuchus, Tropical Longitude: 22°46' Sagittarius, Sidereal Longitude: 28°35' Scorpio, Declination: 12°32'

* Regulus   - Constellation: Leo, Tropical Longitude: 0°09'
Virgo, Sidereal Longitude: 5°58' Leo, Declination: 11°50'

* Acubens   - Constellation: Cancer, Tropical Longitude:
13°58' Leo, Sidereal Longitude: 19°47' Cancer,
Declination: 11°45'

* Vindemiatrix   - Constellation: Virgo, Tropical Longitude:
10°16' Libra, Sidereal Longitude: 16°04' Virgo,
Declination: 10°49'

* Altair   - Constellation: Aquila, Tropical Longitude: 2°06'
Aquarius, Sidereal Longitude: 7°55' Capricorn,
Declination: 8°55'

* Betelgeuse   - Constellation: Orion, Tropical Longitude:
29°05' Gemini, Sidereal Longitude: 4°54' Gemini,
Declination: 7°24'

* Bellatrix   - Constellation: Orion, Tropical Longitude:
21°17' Gemini, Sidereal Longitude: 27°05' Taurus,
Declination: 6°22'

* Procyon   - Constellation: Canis Minor, Tropical
Longitude: 26°07' Cancer, Sidereal Longitude: 1°55'
Cancer, Declination: 5°09'

* Menkar   - Constellation: Cetus, Tropical Longitude:
14°39' Taurus, Sidereal Longitude: 20°28' Aries,
Declination: 4°11'

* Al Rischa   - Constellation: Pisces, Tropical Longitude:
29°42' Aries, Sidereal Longitude: 5°31' Aries, Declination:
2°52'

* Sadalmelek   - Constellation: Aquarius, Tropical Longitude: 3°40' Pisces, Sidereal Longitude: 9°29' Aquarius, Declination: -0°12'

* Alnilam   - Constellation: Orion, Tropical Longitude: 23°48' Gemini, Sidereal Longitude: 29°36' Taurus, Declination: -1°11'

* Sadalsuud   - Constellation: Aquarius, Tropical Longitude: 23°43' Aquarius, Sidereal Longitude: 29°32' Capricorn, Declination: -5°28'

* Rigel   - Constellation: Orion, Tropical Longitude: 17°10' Gemini, Sidereal Longitude: 22°58' Taurus, Declination: -8°10'

* Alphard   - Constellation: Hydra, Tropical Longitude: 27°36' Leo, Sidereal Longitude: 3°25' Leo, Declination: -8°45'

* Zuben Eschamali   - Constellation: Libra, Tropical Longitude: 19°42' Scorpio, Sidereal Longitude: 25°30' Libra, Declination: -9°28'

* Spica   - Constellation: Virgo, Tropical Longitude: 24°10' Libra, Sidereal Longitude: 29°58' Virgo, Declination: -11°17'

* Deneb Algedi   - Constellation: Capricorn, Tropical Longitude: 23°52' Aquarius, Sidereal Longitude: 29°40' Capricorn, Declination: -16°01'

* Zuben Elgenubi   - Constellation: Libra, Tropical Longitude: 15°24' Scorpio, Sidereal Longitude: 21°13' Libra, Declination: -16°08'

* Sirius   - Constellation: Canis Major, Tropical Longitude: 14°25' Cancer, Sidereal Longitude: 20°13' Gemini, Declination: -16°44'

* Alkes   - Constellation: Crater, Tropical Longitude: 24°01' Virgo, Sidereal Longitude: 29°49' Leo, Declination: -18°25'

* Mirzam (Al Murzims)   - Constellation: Canis Major, Tropical Longitude: 7°31' Cancer, Sidereal Longitude: 13°20' Gemini, Declination: -17°58'

* Facies   - Constellation: Sagittarius, Tropical Longitude: 8°38' Capricorn, Sidereal Longitude: 14°27' Sagittarius, Declination: -23°53'

* Antares   - Constellation: Scorpio, Tropical Longitude: 10°05' Sagittarius, Sidereal Longitude: 15°54' Scorpio, Declination: -26°29'

* Fomalhaut   - Constellation: Piscis Austrinus, Tropical Longitude: 4°11' Pisces, Sidereal Longitude: 10°00' Aquarius, Declination: -29°29'

* Aculeus   - Constellation: Scorpio, Tropical Longitude: 26°07' Sagittarius, Sidereal Longitude: 1°55' Sagittarius, Declination: -32°15'

* Acumen   - Constellation: Scorpio, Tropical Longitude: 29°02' Sagittarius, Sidereal Longitude: 4°50' Sagittarius, Declination: -34°47'

* Phact   - Constellation: Columba, Tropical Longitude: 22°30' Gemini, Sidereal Longitude: 28°19' Taurus, Declination: -34°03'

* Rukbat   - Constellation: Sagittarius, Tropical Longitude:
16°57' Capricorn, Sidereal Longitude: 22°46' Sagittarius,
Declination: -40°34'

* Ankaa   - Constellation: Phoenix, Tropical Longitude:
15°49' Pisces, Sidereal Longitude: 21°38' Aquarius,
Declination: -42°10'

* Canopus   - Constellation: Carina, Tropical Longitude:
15°18' Cancer, Sidereal Longitude: 21°07' Gemini,
Declination: -52°42'

* Achernar   - Constellation: Eridanus, Tropical Longitude:
15°38' Pisces, Sidereal Longitude: 21°27' Aquarius,
Declination: -57°07'

* Agena   - Constellation: Centaurus, Tropical Longitude:
24°07' Scorpio, Sidereal Longitude: 29°55' Libra,
Declination: -60°29'

* Toliman   - Constellation: Centaurus, Tropical Longitude:
29°46' Scorpio, Sidereal Longitude: 5°35' Scorpio,
Declination: -60°55'

* Acrux   - Constellation: Crux, Tropical Longitude: 12°11'
Scorpio,
Sidereal Longitude: 18°00' Libra, Declination: -63°13'

JANUARY 2025 CONJUNCTIONS
All times given in UTC (Coordinated Universal Time)

* 01/01/25 - 02:35 PM: Moon with Altair

* 02/01/25 - 05:49 AM: Sun with Diadem

* 02/01/25 - 02:17 PM: Mercury with Arcturus

* 02/01/25 - 05:59 PM: Moon with Sualocin

* 03/01/25 - 04:29 AM: Moon with Sadalsuud

* 03/01/25 - 04:42 AM: Moon with Deneb Algedi

* 03/01/25 - 05:48 AM: Sun with Vindemiatrix

* 03/01/25 - 09:44 PM: Moon with Sadalmelek

* 03/01/25 - 10:38 PM: Moon with Fomalhaut

* 04/01/25 - 01:08 AM: Moon with Deneb Adige

* 04/01/25 - 06:23 PM: Moon with Achernar

* 04/01/25 - 06:42 PM: Moon with Ankaa

* 05/01/25 - 08:25 AM: Moon with Markab

* 05/01/25 - 04:09 PM: Mercury with Aculeus

* 05/01/25 - 05:36 PM: Sun with Vega

* 05/01/25 - 06:30 PM: Moon with Scheat

* 06/01/25 - 07:04 AM: Venus with Fomalhaut

* 06/01/25 - 08:03 PM: Moon with Alpheraz

* 07/01/25 - 07:14 PM: Mercury with Acumen

* 07/01/25 - 09:49 PM: Moon with Alrischa

* 07/01/25 - 11:28 PM: Moon with Mirach

* 08/01/25   - 11:47 AM: Moon with Hamal

* 08/01/25   - 11:59 AM: Moon with Schedir

* 08/01/25   - 11:06 PM: Moon with Menkar

* 09/01/25   - 03:48 PM: Moon with Capulus

* 09/01/25   - 07:10 PM: Moon with Algol

* 10/01/25   - 01:41 AM: Moon with Alcyone

* 10/01/25   - 05:13 AM: Moon with Mirfach

* 10/01/25   - 06:21 PM: Moon with Aldebaran

* 11/01/25   - 06:21 AM: Moon with Rigel

* 11/01/25   - 01:24 PM: Moon with Bellatrix

* 11/01/25   - 02:59 PM: Moon with Capella

* 11/01/25   - 03:31 PM: Moon with Phact

* 11/01/25   - 04:12 PM: Moon with El Nath

* 11/01/25   - 05:43 PM: Moon with Alnilam

* 11/01/25   - 11:41 PM: Moon with Alkaid

* 12/01/25   - 02:51 AM: Moon with Betelgeuse

* 12/01/25   - 05:28 PM: Moon with Mirzam

* 12/01/25   - 08:49 PM: Moon with Alhena

* 13/01/25   - 05:30 AM: Moon with Sirius

* 13/01/25   - 07:05 AM: Moon with Canopus

* 13/01/25   - 11:33 AM: North Node with Scheat

* 13/01/25   - 04:23 PM: Moon with Castor

* 13/01/25   - 09:39 PM: Moon with Pollux

* 14/01/25   - 02:14 AM: Moon with Procyon

* 14/01/25 - 09:18 AM: Mercury with Facies
* 15/01/25 - 10:42 AM: Moon with Acubens
* 15/01/25 - 08:05 PM: Mercury with Acrux
* 16/01/25 - 12:14 PM: Moon with Alphard
* 16/01/25 - 05:05 PM: Moon with Regulus
* 16/01/25 - 07:46 PM: Sun with Arcturus
* 17/01/25 - 07:27 AM: Sun with Spica
* 17/01/25 - 03:14 PM: Moon with Zosma
* 18/01/25 - 11:30 AM: Moon with Denebola
* 18/01/25 - 01:08 PM: Mars with Procyon
* 18/01/25 - 02:29 PM: Venus with Achernar
* 18/01/25 - 03:36 PM: Moon with Alkes
* 18/01/25 - 07:06 PM: Venus with Ankaa
* 19/01/25 - 12:12 AM: Mercury with Vega
* 19/01/25 - 10:16 PM: Moon with Diadem
* 20/01/25 - 12:15 AM: Moon with Vindemiatrix
* 21/01/25 - 04:29 AM: Moon with Spica
* 21/01/25 - 05:18 AM: Moon with Arcturus
* 21/01/25 - 10:05 PM: Sun with Altair
* 22/01/25 - 05:02 PM: Moon with Acrux
* 22/01/25 - 05:55 PM: Moon with Alphecca
* 22/01/25 - 11:30 PM: Moon with Zuben Elgenubi
* 23/01/25 - 08:05 AM: Moon with Zuben Eschamali
* 23/01/25 - 04:52 PM: Moon with Agena

* 24/01/25   - 04:04 AM: Moon with Toliman

* 24/01/25   - 05:24 AM: Mercury with Agena

* 25/01/25   - 12:09 AM: Moon with Antares

* 25/01/25   - 07:07 AM: Mars with Pollux

* 25/01/25   - 12:22 PM: Moon with Ras Algethi

* 26/01/25   - 12:16 AM: Moon with Ras Alhague

* 26/01/25   - 06:30 AM: Moon with Aculeus

* 26/01/25   - 12:56 PM: Moon with Acumen

* 26/01/25   - 02:07 PM: Venus with Markab

* 27/01/25   - 05:34 AM: Moon with Facies

* 27/01/25   - 06:09 PM: Moon with Vega

* 27/01/25   - 08:32 PM: Moon with Rukbat

* 28/01/25   - 11:13 PM: Moon with Altair

* 29/01/25   - 10:10 AM: Mercury with Altair

* 30/01/25   - 02:04 AM: Moon with Sualocin

* 30/01/25   - 12:17 PM: Moon with Sadalsuud

* 30/01/25   - 12:31 PM: Moon with Deneb Algedi

* 31/01/25   - 05:05 AM: Moon with Sadalmelek

* 31/01/25   - 05:57 AM: Moon with Fomalhaut

* 31/01/25   - 08:23 AM: Moon with Deneb Adige

FEBRUARY 2025 CONJUNCTIONS
All times given in UTC (Coordinated Universal Time)

* 01/02/25   - 01:28 AM: Moon with Ankaa

* 01/02/25   - 02:50 PM: Moon with Markab

* 02/02/25   - 12:40 AM: Moon with Scheat

* 03/02/25   - 01:43 AM: Moon with Alpheraz

* 03/02/25   - 04:42 PM: Mars with Castor

* 03/02/25   - 10:30 PM: Venus with Scheat

* 04/02/25   - 03:12 AM: Moon with Alrischa

* 04/02/25   - 04:50 AM: Moon with Mirach

* 04/02/25   - 05:07 PM: Moon with Hamal

* 04/02/25   - 05:19 PM: Moon with Schedir

* 05/02/25   - 04:27 AM: Moon with Menkar

* 05/02/25   - 09:18 PM: Moon with Capulus

* 06/02/25   - 12:43 AM: Moon with Algol

* 06/02/25   - 06:40 AM: Sun with Sualocin

* 06/02/25   - 07:18 AM: Moon with Alcyone

* 06/02/25   - 10:54 AM: Moon with Mirfach

* 07/02/25   - 12:16 AM: Moon with Aldebaran

* 07/02/25   - 12:31 PM: Moon with Rigel

* 07/02/25   - 03:34 PM: Mercury with Sualocin

* 07/02/25   - 07:44 PM: Moon with Bellatrix

* 07/02/25   - 09:20 PM: Moon with Capella

* 07/02/25   - 09:53 PM: Moon with Phact
* 07/02/25   - 10:36 PM: Moon with El Nath
* 08/02/25   - 12:09 AM: Moon with Alnilam
* 08/02/25   - 06:15 AM: Moon with Alkaid
* 08/02/25   - 09:29 AM: Moon with Betelgeuse
* 09/02/25   - 12:27 AM: Moon with Mirzam
* 09/02/25   - 03:52 AM: Moon with Alhena
* 09/02/25   - 12:46 PM: Moon with Sirius
* 09/02/25   - 02:23 PM: Moon with Canopus
* 09/02/25   - 11:53 PM: Moon with Castor
* 10/02/25   - 05:15 AM: Moon with Pollux
* 10/02/25   - 09:55 AM: Moon with Procyon
* 11/02/25   - 01:10 AM: Mercury with Sadalsuud
* 11/02/25   - 02:57 AM: Mercury with Deneb Algedi
* 11/02/25   - 11:12 AM: Mercury with Achernar
* 11/02/25   - 06:52 PM: Moon with Acubens
* 12/02/25   - 05:21 AM: Sun with Sadalsuud
* 12/02/25   - 08:31 AM: Sun with Deneb Algedi
* 12/02/25   - 08:35 PM: Moon with Alphard
* 13/02/25   - 01:27 AM: Moon with Regulus
* 13/02/25   - 11:36 PM: Moon with Zosma
* 14/02/25   - 07:47 PM: Moon with Denebola
* 14/02/25   - 11:52 PM: Moon with Alkes
* 16/02/25   - 06:21 AM: Moon with Diadem

* 16/02/25 - 07:31 AM: Mercury with Fomalhaut

* 16/02/25 - 08:20 AM: Moon with Vindemiatrix

* 17/02/25 - 12:28 PM: Moon with Spica

* 17/02/25 - 01:17 PM: Moon with Arcturus

* 17/02/25 - 01:48 PM: Mercury with Deneb Adige

* 19/02/25 - 01:06 AM: Moon with Acrux

* 19/02/25 - 01:59 AM: Moon with Alphecca

* 19/02/25 - 07:37 AM: Moon with Zuben Elgenubi

* 19/02/25 - 04:16 PM: Moon with Zuben Eschamali

* 20/02/25 - 01:09 AM: Moon with Agena

* 20/02/25 - 05:28 AM: Sun with Alcyone

* 20/02/25 - 12:29 PM: Moon with Toliman

* 21/02/25 - 08:53 AM: Moon with Antares

* 21/02/25 - 05:17 PM: Sun with Fomalhaut

* 21/02/25 - 09:20 PM: Moon with Ras Algethi

* 22/02/25 - 09:28 AM: Moon with Ras Alhague

* 22/02/25 - 03:49 PM: Moon with Aculeus

* 22/02/25 - 10:20 PM: Moon with Acumen

* 23/02/25 - 01:35 AM: Mercury with Ankaa

* 23/02/25 - 03:16 PM: Moon with Facies

* 24/02/25 - 12:53 AM: Sun with Deneb Adige

* 24/02/25 - 04:02 AM: Moon with Vega

* 24/02/25 - 06:27 AM: Moon with Rukbat

* 25/02/25 - 09:22 AM: Moon with Altair

* 26/02/25   - 12:11 PM: Moon with Sualocin

* 26/02/25   - 10:20 PM: Moon with Sadalsuud

* 26/02/25   - 10:33 PM: Moon with Deneb Algedi

* 27/02/25   - 12:31 AM: Mercury with Markab

* 27/02/25   - 02:53 PM: Moon with Sadalmelek

* 27/02/25   - 03:44 PM: Moon with Fomalhaut

* 27/02/25   - 06:08 PM: Moon with Deneb Adige

* 28/02/25   - 10:32 AM: Moon with Achernar

* 28/02/25   - 10:50 AM: Moon with Ankaa

* 28/02/25   - 11:50 PM: Moon with Markab

MARCH 2025 CONJUNCTIONS
All times given in UTC (Coordinated Universal Time)

* 01/03/25   - 09:23 AM: Moon with Scheat

* 02/03/25   - 09:37 AM: Moon with Alpheraz

* 03/03/25   - 04:21 AM: Mercury with Scheat

* 03/03/25   - 10:16 AM: Moon with Alrischa

* 03/03/25   - 11:51 AM: Moon with Mirach

* 03/03/25   - 11:45 PM: Moon with Hamal

* 03/03/25   - 11:57 PM: Moon with Schedir

* 04/03/25   - 10:47 AM: Moon with Menkar

* 05/03/25   - 03:14 AM: Moon with Capulus

* 05/03/25   - 06:35 AM: Moon with Algol

* 05/03/25   - 01:04 PM: Moon with Alcyone

* 05/03/25   - 04:36 PM: Moon with Mirfach

* 05/03/25   - 11:54 PM: Sun with Achernar

* 06/03/25   - 04:18 AM: Sun with Ankaa

* 06/03/25   - 05:47 AM: Moon with Aldebaran

* 06/03/25   - 05:57 PM: Moon with Rigel

* 07/03/25   - 01:08 AM: Moon with Bellatrix

* 07/03/25   - 02:44 AM: Moon with Capella

* 07/03/25   - 03:17 AM: Moon with Phact

* 07/03/25   - 03:59 AM: Moon with El Nath

* 07/03/25   - 05:32 AM: Moon with Alnilam

* 07/03/25   - 11:39 AM: Moon with Alkaid

* 07/03/25   - 02:53 PM: Moon with Betelgeuse

* 08/03/25   - 05:56 AM: Moon with Mirzam

* 08/03/25   - 09:23 AM: Moon with Alhena

* 08/03/25   - 06:22 PM: Moon with Sirius

* 08/03/25   - 08:00 PM: Moon with Canopus

* 09/03/25   - 05:37 AM: Moon with Castor

* 09/03/25   - 11:04 AM: Moon with Pollux

* 09/03/25   - 03:48 PM: Moon with Procyon

* 11/03/25   - 01:15 AM: Moon with Acubens

* 12/03/25   - 03:20 AM: Moon with Alphard

* 12/03/25   - 08:16 AM: Moon with Regulus

* 13/03/25   - 06:39 AM: Moon with Zosma

* 13/03/25   - 06:50 AM: Sun with Markab

* 14/03/25   - 02:58 AM: Moon with Denebola

* 14/03/25   - 07:04 AM: Moon with Alkes

* 15/03/25   - 01:36 PM: Moon with Diadem

* 15/03/25   - 03:35 PM: Moon with Vindemiatrix

* 16/03/25   - 07:41 PM: Moon with Spica

* 16/03/25   - 08:29 PM: Moon with Arcturus

* 18/03/25   - 02:24 AM: Mars with Castor

* 18/03/25   - 08:18 AM: Moon with Acrux

* 18/03/25   - 09:11 AM: Moon with Alphecca

* 18/03/25   - 02:49 PM: Moon with Zuben Elgenubi

* 18/03/25   - 11:30 PM: Moon with Zuben Eschamali
* 19/03/25   - 07:10 AM: Saturn with Markab
* 19/03/25   - 08:26 AM: Moon with Agena
* 19/03/25   - 07:51 PM: Moon with Toliman
* 20/03/25   - 02:00 AM: Sun with Scheat
* 20/03/25   - 04:30 PM: Moon with Antares
* 21/03/25   - 05:08 AM: Moon with Ras Algethi
* 21/03/25   - 05:30 PM: Moon with Ras Alhague
* 21/03/25   - 11:59 PM: Moon with Aculeus
* 22/03/25   - 06:37 AM: Moon with Acumen
* 22/03/25   - 07:07 PM: Neptune with Scheat
* 23/03/25   - 12:00 AM: Moon with Facies
* 23/03/25   - 01:07 PM: Moon with Vega
* 23/03/25   - 03:35 PM: Moon with Rukbat
* 24/03/25   - 07:13 PM: Moon with Altair
* 25/03/25   - 10:38 PM: Moon with Sualocin
* 26/03/25   - 08:56 AM: Moon with Sadalsuud
* 26/03/25   - 09:10 AM: Moon with Deneb Algedi
* 26/03/25   - 07:21 PM: Uranus with Capulus
* 27/03/25   - 01:42 AM: Moon with Sadalmelek
* 27/03/25   - 02:33 AM: Moon with Fomalhaut
* 27/03/25   - 04:58 AM: Moon with Deneb Adige
* 27/03/25   - 08:39 PM: Venus with Scheat
* 27/03/25   - 09:25 PM: Moon with Achernar

* 27/03/25   - 09:43 PM: Moon with Ankaa
* 28/03/25   - 10:40 AM: Moon with Markab
* 28/03/25   - 08:08 PM: Moon with Scheat
* 29/03/25   - 02:11 AM: Mars with Pollux
* 29/03/25   - 07:56 PM: Moon with Alpheraz
* 30/03/25   - 12:05 PM: Mercury with Scheat
* 30/03/25   - 07:56 PM: Moon with Alrischa
* 30/03/25   - 09:28 PM: Moon with Mirach
* 31/03/25   - 08:59 AM: Moon with Hamal
* 31/03/25   - 09:10 AM: Moon with Schedir
* 31/03/25   - 07:38 PM: Moon with Menkar

APRIL 2025 CONJUNCTIONS
All times given in UTC (Coordinated Universal Time)

* 01/04/25   - 11:30 AM: Moon with Capulus

* 01/04/25   - 02:44 PM: Moon with Algol

* 01/04/25   - 08:59 PM: Moon with Alcyone

* 02/04/25   - 12:23 AM: Moon with Mirfach

* 02/04/25   - 01:08 PM: Moon with Aldebaran

* 03/04/25   - 12:12 AM: Jupiter with Rigel

* 03/04/25   - 12:55 AM: Moon with Rigel

* 03/04/25   - 07:53 AM: Moon with Bellatrix

* 03/04/25   - 09:27 AM: Moon with Capella

* 03/04/25   - 09:59 AM: Moon with Phact

* 03/04/25   - 10:40 AM: Moon with El Nath

* 03/04/25   - 12:10 PM: Moon with Alnilam

* 03/04/25   - 06:07 PM: Moon with Alkaid

* 03/04/25   - 09:17 PM: Moon with Betelgeuse

* 04/04/25   - 04:31 AM: Sun with Alpheraz

* 04/04/25   - 12:00 PM: Moon with Mirzam

* 04/04/25   - 03:23 PM: Moon with Alhena

* 05/04/25   - 12:13 AM: Moon with Sirius

* 05/04/25 - 01:50 AM: Moon with Canopus

* 05/04/25 - 11:20 AM: Moon with Castor

* 05/04/25 - 04:44 PM: Moon with Pollux

* 05/04/25 - 07:35 PM: Mars with Procyon

* 05/04/25 - 09:25 PM: Moon with Procyon

* 07/04/25 - 06:49 AM: Moon with Acubens

* 08/04/25 - 09:02 AM: Moon with Alphard

* 08/04/25 - 02:00 PM: Moon with Regulus

* 09/04/25 - 12:34 PM: Moon with Zosma

* 10/04/25 - 09:04 AM: Moon with Denebola

* 10/04/25 - 01:12 PM: Moon with Alkes

* 11/04/25 - 07:55 PM: Moon with Diadem

* 11/04/25 - 09:55 PM: Moon with Vindemiatrix

* 13/04/25 - 02:04 AM: Moon with Spica

* 13/04/25 - 02:53 AM: Moon with Arcturus

* 14/04/25 - 02:40 PM: Moon with Acrux

* 14/04/25 - 03:33 PM: Moon with Alphecca

* 14/04/25 - 09:11 PM: Moon with Zuben Elgenubi

* 15/04/25 - 05:51 AM: Moon with Zuben Eschamali

* 15/04/25 - 02:47 PM: Moon with Agena

* 15/04/25 - 07:58 PM: Mercury with Scheat

* 16/04/25   - 02:12 AM: Moon with Toliman

* 16/04/25   - 10:53 PM: Moon with Antares

* 17/04/25   - 11:35 AM: Moon with Ras Algethi

* 18/04/25   - 12:03 AM: Moon with Ras Alhague

* 18/04/25   - 06:37 AM: Moon with Aculeus

* 18/04/25   - 11:14 AM: Uranus with Algol

* 18/04/25   - 01:19 PM: Moon with Acumen

* 19/04/25   - 04:37 AM: Sun with Mirach

* 19/04/25   - 07:00 AM: Moon with Facies

* 19/04/25   - 01:13 PM: Sun with Al Rischa

* 19/04/25   - 08:23 PM: Moon with Vega

* 19/04/25   - 10:55 PM: Moon with Rukbat

* 21/04/25   - 03:17 AM: Moon with Altair

* 22/04/25   - 07:33 AM: Moon with Sualocin

* 22/04/25   - 06:12 PM: Moon with Sadalsuud

* 22/04/25   - 06:26 PM: Moon with Deneb Algedi

* 23/04/25   - 11:28 AM: Moon with Sadalmelek

* 23/04/25   - 12:21 PM: Moon with Fomalhaut

* 23/04/25   - 02:50 PM: Moon with Deneb Adige

* 24/04/25   - 07:45 AM: Moon with Achernar

* 24/04/25   - 08:03 AM: Moon with Ankaa

* 24/04/25   - 09:17 PM: Moon with Markab

* 25/04/25   - 06:55 AM: Moon with Scheat

* 26/04/25   - 06:59 AM: Moon with Alpheraz

* 27/04/25   - 06:57 AM: Moon with Alrischa

* 27/04/25   - 08:28 AM: Moon with Mirach

* 27/04/25   - 07:52 PM: Moon with Hamal

* 27/04/25   - 08:03 PM: Moon with Schedir

* 28/04/25   - 01:10 AM: Sun with Hamal

* 28/04/25   - 04:04 AM: Sun with Schedir (Schedar)

* 28/04/25   - 06:21 AM: Moon with Menkar

* 28/04/25   - 09:53 PM: Moon with Capulus

* 29/04/25   - 01:02 AM: Moon with Algol

* 29/04/25   - 07:07 AM: Moon with Alcyone

* 29/04/25   - 10:26 AM: Moon with Mirfach

* 29/04/25   - 10:48 PM: Moon with Aldebaran

* 30/04/25   - 04:36 AM: Venus with Scheat

* 30/04/25   - 08:50 AM: Mercury with Alpheraz

* 30/04/25   - 10:12 AM: Moon with Rigel

* 30/04/25   - 02:55 PM: Jupiter with Bellatrix

* 30/04/25   - 04:56 PM: Moon with Bellatrix

* 30/04/25   - 06:26 PM: Moon with Capella

* 30/04/25 - 06:58 PM: Moon with Phact

* 30/04/25 - 07:37 PM: Moon with El Nath

* 30/04/25 - 09:05 PM: Moon with Alnilam

MAY 2025 CONJUNCTIONS
All times given in UTC (Coordinated Universal Time)

* 01/05/25 - 02:49 AM: Moon with Alkaid

* 01/05/25 - 05:53 AM: Moon with Betelgeuse

* 01/05/25 - 08:06 PM: Moon with Mirzam

* 01/05/25 - 11:23 PM: Moon with Alhena

* 02/05/25 - 07:56 AM: Moon with Sirius

* 02/05/25 - 09:30 AM: Moon with Canopus

* 02/05/25 - 06:43 PM: Moon with Castor

* 02/05/25 - 11:57 PM: Moon with Pollux

* 03/05/25 - 04:31 AM: Moon with Procyon

* 04/05/25 - 01:11 PM: Moon with Acubens

* 04/05/25 - 09:58 PM: Sun with Menkar

* 05/05/25 - 03:36 AM: Jupiter with Capella

* 05/05/25 - 03:04 PM: Moon with Alphard

* 05/05/25 - 08:00 PM: Moon with Regulus

* 06/05/25 - 04:34 PM: Jupiter with Phact

* 06/05/25 - 06:28 PM: Moon with Zosma

* 07/05/25 - 02:57 PM: Moon with Denebola

* 07/05/25 - 07:05 PM: Moon with Alkes

* 08/05/25 - 02:55 PM: Jupiter with El Nath

* 09/05/25 - 01:54 AM: Moon with Diadem

* 09/05/25 - 03:53 AM: Moon with Vindemiatrix

* 10/05/25 - 03:20 AM: Mercury with Mirach

* 10/05/25   - 08:08 AM: Moon with Spica

* 10/05/25   - 08:22 AM: Mercury with Al Rischa

* 10/05/25   - 08:56 AM: Moon with Arcturus

* 11/05/25   - 08:44 PM: Moon with Acrux

* 11/05/25   - 09:37 PM: Moon with Alphecca

* 12/05/25   - 03:14 AM: Moon with Zuben Elgenubi

* 12/05/25   - 11:53 AM: Moon with Zuben Eschamali

* 12/05/25   - 07:54 PM: Jupiter with Alnilam

* 12/05/25   - 08:47 PM: Moon with Agena

* 13/05/25   - 08:09 AM: Moon with Toliman

* 14/05/25   - 04:45 AM: Moon with Antares

* 14/05/25   - 05:25 PM: Moon with Ras Algethi

* 15/05/25   - 01:41 AM: Mercury with Hamal

* 15/05/25   - 02:34 AM: Sun with Capulus

* 15/05/25   - 03:13 AM: Mercury with Schedir (Schedar)

* 15/05/25   - 05:50 AM: Moon with Ras Alhague

* 15/05/25   - 12:23 PM: Moon with Aculeus

* 15/05/25   - 07:05 PM: Moon with Acumen

* 16/05/25   - 05:57 AM: Sun with Algol

* 16/05/25   - 12:47 PM: Moon with Facies

* 17/05/25   - 02:14 AM: Moon with Vega

* 17/05/25   - 04:47 AM: Moon with Rukbat

* 18/05/25   - 09:28 AM: Moon with Altair

* 18/05/25   - 09:30 AM: Mars with Acubens

* 18/05/25   - 02:19 PM: Mercury with Menkar

* 19/05/25   - 02:19 PM: Moon with Sualocin

* 20/05/25   - 01:15 AM: Moon with Sadalsuud

* 20/05/25   - 01:29 AM: Moon with Deneb Algedi

* 20/05/25   - 07:02 PM: Moon with Sadalmelek

* 20/05/25   - 07:09 PM: Venus with Alpheraz

* 20/05/25   - 07:57 PM: Moon with Fomalhaut

* 20/05/25   - 10:30 PM: Moon with Deneb Adige

* 21/05/25   - 10:27 AM: Saturn with Scheat

* 21/05/25   - 03:58 PM: Moon with Achernar

* 21/05/25   - 04:17 PM: Moon with Ankaa

* 22/05/25   - 05:59 AM: Moon with Markab

* 22/05/25   - 03:56 PM: Moon with Scheat

* 23/05/25   - 07:30 AM: Sun with Mirfach

* 23/05/25   - 11:10 AM: Mercury with Capulus

* 23/05/25   - 04:45 PM: Moon with Alpheraz

* 23/05/25   - 11:45 PM: Mercury with Algol

* 24/05/25   - 05:18 PM: Moon with Alrischa

* 24/05/25   - 06:51 PM: Moon with Mirach

* 25/05/25   - 06:27 AM: Moon with Hamal

* 25/05/25   - 06:38 AM: Moon with Schedir

* 25/05/25   - 06:58 AM: Mercury with Alcyone

* 25/05/25   - 05:03 PM: Moon with Menkar

* 26/05/25   - 08:40 AM: Moon with Capulus

* 26/05/25   - 11:49 AM: Moon with Algol

* 26/05/25   - 05:54 PM: Moon with Alcyone

* 26/05/25   - 09:12 PM: Moon with Mirfach

* 27/05/25   - 03:56 AM: Mercury with Mirfach

* 27/05/25   - 09:29 AM: Moon with Aldebaran

* 27/05/25   - 08:45 PM: Moon with Rigel

* 28/05/25   - 03:23 AM: Moon with Bellatrix

* 28/05/25   - 04:52 AM: Moon with Capella

* 28/05/25   - 05:22 AM: Moon with Phact

* 28/05/25   - 06:01 AM: Moon with El Nath

* 28/05/25   - 07:27 AM: Moon with Alnilam

* 28/05/25   - 01:05 PM: Moon with Alkaid

* 28/05/25   - 04:05 PM: Moon with Betelgeuse

* 29/05/25   - 05:59 AM: Moon with Mirzam

* 29/05/25   - 09:10 AM: Moon with Alhena

* 29/05/25   - 05:30 PM: Moon with Sirius

* 29/05/25   - 07:01 PM: Moon with Canopus

* 30/05/25   - 03:59 AM: Moon with Castor

* 30/05/25   - 06:50 AM: Mercury with Aldebaran

* 30/05/25   - 09:05 AM: Moon with Pollux

* 30/05/25   - 10:13 AM: Sun with Aldebaran

* 30/05/25   - 01:31 PM: Moon with Procyon

* 31/05/25   - 09:16 PM: Moon with Acubens

JUNE 2025 CONJUNCTIONS
All times given in UTC (Coordinated Universal Time)

* 01/06/25 - 10:31 PM: Moon with Alphard

* 02/06/25 - 12:34 AM: Jupiter with Betelgeuse

* 02/06/25 - 03:20 AM: Moon with Regulus

* 02/06/25 - 11:41 AM: Mercury with Rigel

* 03/06/25 - 01:23 AM: Moon with Zosma

* 03/06/25 - 09:37 PM: Moon with Denebola

* 04/06/25 - 01:43 AM: Moon with Alkes

* 04/06/25 - 07:04 PM: Mercury with Bellatrix

* 05/06/25 - 05:20 AM: Mercury with Capella

* 05/06/25 - 08:20 AM: Moon with Diadem

* 05/06/25 - 08:54 AM: Mercury with Phact

* 05/06/25 - 10:20 AM: Moon with Vindemiatrix

* 05/06/25 - 01:25 PM: Mercury with El Nath

* 05/06/25 - 10:09 PM: Venus with Al Rischa

* 05/06/25 - 11:24 PM: Mercury with Alnilam

* 06/06/25 - 02:32 PM: Moon with Spica

* 06/06/25 - 03:21 PM: Moon with Arcturus

* 06/06/25 - 06:26 PM: Sun with Rigel

* 08/06/25 - 02:10 AM: Mercury with Betelgeuse

* 08/06/25 - 03:09 AM: Moon with Acrux

* 08/06/25 - 04:01 AM: Moon with Alphecca

* 08/06/25 - 09:39 AM: Moon with Zuben Elgenubi

* 08/06/25 - 06:17 PM: Moon with Zuben Eschamali

* 09/06/25 - 03:10 AM: Moon with Agena

* 09/06/25 - 02:31 PM: Moon with Toliman

* 10/06/25 - 11:00 AM: Moon with Antares

* 10/06/25 - 11:35 PM: Moon with Ras Algethi

* 11/06/25 - 11:55 AM: Moon with Ras Alhague

* 11/06/25 - 06:24 PM: Moon with Aculeus

* 11/06/25 - 10:21 PM: North Node with Markab

* 11/06/25 - 11:57 PM: Sun with Bellatrix

* 12/06/25 - 01:03 AM: Moon with Acumen

* 12/06/25 - 06:35 PM: Moon with Facies

* 12/06/25 - 07:22 PM: Mercury with Mirzam (Al Murzims)

* 12/06/25 - 10:59 PM: Sun with Capella

* 13/06/25 - 02:19 AM: Mars with Alphard

* 13/06/25 - 06:56 AM: Sun with Phact

* 13/06/25 - 07:55 AM: Moon with Vega

* 13/06/25 - 10:27 AM: Moon with Rukbat

* 13/06/25 - 04:59 PM: Sun with El Nath

* 13/06/25 - 08:00 PM: Mercury with Alhena

* 14/06/25 - 02:35 AM: Venus with Hamal

* 14/06/25 - 05:18 AM: Venus with Schedir (Schedar)

* 14/06/25 - 02:58 PM: Moon with Altair

* 14/06/25 - 03:11 PM: Sun with Alnilam

* 15/06/25   - 07:50 PM: Moon with Sualocin

* 16/06/25   - 02:20 AM: Mercury with Sirius

* 16/06/25   - 02:21 AM: Mars with Regulus

* 16/06/25   - 06:49 AM: Moon with Sadalsuud

* 16/06/25   - 07:03 AM: Moon with Deneb Algedi

* 16/06/25   - 02:42 PM: Mercury with Canopus

* 17/06/25   - 12:47 AM: Moon with Sadalmelek

* 17/06/25   - 01:43 AM: Moon with Fomalhaut

* 17/06/25   - 04:19 AM: Moon with Deneb Adige

* 17/06/25   - 10:05 PM: Moon with Achernar

* 17/06/25   - 10:24 PM: Moon with Ankaa

* 18/06/25   - 12:25 PM: Moon with Markab

* 18/06/25   - 10:38 PM: Moon with Scheat

* 19/06/25   - 06:12 AM: Sun with Betelgeuse

* 19/06/25   - 06:14 PM: Mercury with Castor

* 20/06/25   - 12:11 AM: Moon with Alpheraz

* 20/06/25   - 11:34 AM: Venus with Menkar

* 21/06/25   - 01:32 AM: Moon with Alrischa

* 21/06/25   - 03:08 AM: Moon with Mirach

* 21/06/25   - 03:06 PM: Moon with Hamal

* 21/06/25   - 03:17 PM: Moon with Schedir

* 21/06/25   - 03:36 PM: Mercury with Pollux

* 22/06/25   - 02:01 AM: Moon with Menkar

* 22/06/25   - 06:04 PM: Moon with Capulus

* 22/06/25   - 09:17 PM: Moon with Algol

* 23/06/25   - 03:30 AM: Moon with Alcyone

* 23/06/25   - 06:53 AM: Moon with Mirfach

* 23/06/25   - 08:48 AM: Mercury with Procyon

* 23/06/25   - 07:23 PM: Moon with Aldebaran

* 24/06/25   - 06:48 AM: Moon with Rigel

* 24/06/25   - 01:30 PM: Moon with Bellatrix

* 24/06/25   - 02:59 PM: Moon with Capella

* 24/06/25   - 03:30 PM: Moon with Phact

* 24/06/25   - 04:10 PM: Moon with El Nath

* 24/06/25   - 05:36 PM: Moon with Alnilam

* 24/06/25   - 11:16 PM: Moon with Alkaid

* 25/06/25   - 02:16 AM: Moon with Betelgeuse

* 25/06/25   - 04:10 PM: Moon with Mirzam

* 25/06/25   - 07:21 PM: Moon with Alhena

* 26/06/25   - 12:17 AM: Uranus with Alcyone

* 26/06/25   - 03:38 AM: Moon with Sirius

* 26/06/25   - 05:08 AM: Moon with Canopus

* 26/06/25   - 02:01 PM: Moon with Castor

* 26/06/25   - 07:03 PM: Moon with Pollux

* 26/06/25   - 11:26 PM: Moon with Procyon

* 28/06/25   - 06:37 AM: Moon with Acubens

* 29/06/25   - 12:30 AM: Sun with Mirzam (Al Murzims)

* 29/06/25   - 07:20 AM: Moon with Alphard

* 29/06/25 - 12:03 PM: Moon with Regulus

* 29/06/25 - 03:39 PM: Venus with Capulus

* 30/06/25 - 09:39 AM: Moon with Zosma

* 30/06/25 - 03:52 PM: Venus with Algol

JULY 2025 CONJUNCTIONS
All times given in UTC (Coordinated Universal Time)

* 01/07/25 - 12:43 AM: Sun with Alhena
* 01/07/25 - 05:30 AM: Moon with Denebola
* 01/07/25 - 09:32 AM: Moon with Alkes
* 02/07/25 - 03:45 PM: Moon with Diadem
* 02/07/25 - 05:43 PM: Moon with Vindemiatrix
* 03/07/25 - 09:45 PM: Moon with Spica
* 03/07/25 - 10:33 PM: Moon with Arcturus
* 04/07/25 - 03:49 AM: Venus with Alcyone
* 05/07/25 - 07:30 AM: Sun with Sirius
* 05/07/25 - 10:18 AM: Moon with Acrux
* 05/07/25 - 11:11 AM: Moon with Alphecca
* 05/07/25 - 04:49 PM: Moon with Zuben Elgenubi
* 06/07/25 - 01:27 AM: Moon with Zuben Eschamali
* 06/07/25 - 06:10 AM: Sun with Canopus
* 06/07/25 - 10:20 AM: Moon with Agena
* 06/07/25 - 08:20 PM: Venus with Mirfach
* 06/07/25 - 09:41 PM: Moon with Toliman
* 07/07/25 - 04:19 PM: Mars with Zosma
* 07/07/25 - 06:11 PM: Moon with Antares
* 08/07/25 - 06:43 AM: Moon with Ras Algethi
* 08/07/25 - 07:00 PM: Moon with Ras Alhague
* 09/07/25 - 01:27 AM: Moon with Aculeus

* 09/07/25 - 08:04 AM: Moon with Acumen

* 10/07/25 - 01:27 AM: Moon with Facies

* 10/07/25 - 02:38 PM: Moon with Vega

* 10/07/25 - 05:08 PM: Moon with Rukbat

* 11/07/25 - 06:46 PM: Sun with Castor

* 11/07/25 - 08:21 PM: Mercury with Acubens

* 11/07/25 - 09:16 PM: Moon with Altair

* 12/07/25 - 11:27 PM: Venus with Aldebaran

* 13/07/25 - 01:31 AM: Jupiter with Mirzam (Al Murzims)

* 13/07/25 - 01:43 AM: Moon with Sualocin

* 13/07/25 - 12:33 PM: Moon with Sadalsuud

* 13/07/25 - 12:47 PM: Moon with Deneb Algedi

* 14/07/25 - 06:20 AM: Moon with Sadalmelek

* 14/07/25 - 07:15 AM: Moon with Fomalhaut

* 14/07/25 - 09:49 AM: Moon with Deneb Adige

* 14/07/25 - 09:26 PM: Sun with Pollux

* 15/07/25 - 03:29 AM: Moon with Achernar

* 15/07/25 - 03:48 AM: Moon with Ankaa

* 15/07/25 - 05:47 PM: Moon with Markab

* 16/07/25 - 04:02 AM: Moon with Scheat

* 17/07/25 - 05:50 AM: Moon with Alpheraz

* 17/07/25 - 02:02 PM: Sun with Procyon

* 18/07/25 - 07:38 AM: Moon with Alrischa

* 18/07/25 - 09:16 AM: Moon with Mirach

* 18/07/25 - 09:31 PM: Moon with Hamal

* 18/07/25 - 09:43 PM: Moon with Schedir

* 19/07/25 - 05:01 AM: Venus with Rigel

* 19/07/25 - 08:44 AM: Moon with Menkar

* 20/07/25 - 01:13 AM: Moon with Capulus

* 20/07/25 - 04:32 AM: Moon with Algol

* 20/07/25 - 10:56 AM: Moon with Alcyone

* 20/07/25 - 02:25 PM: Moon with Mirfach

* 21/07/25 - 03:16 AM: Moon with Aldebaran

* 21/07/25 - 03:00 PM: Moon with Rigel

* 21/07/25 - 04:02 PM: Jupiter with Alhena

* 21/07/25 - 09:52 PM: Moon with Bellatrix

* 21/07/25 - 11:24 PM: Moon with Capella

* 21/07/25 - 11:56 PM: Moon with Phact

* 22/07/25 - 12:36 AM: Moon with El Nath

* 22/07/25 - 02:04 AM: Moon with Alnilam

* 22/07/25 - 07:52 AM: Moon with Alkaid

* 22/07/25 - 10:57 AM: Moon with Betelgeuse

* 23/07/25 - 01:07 AM: Moon with Mirzam

* 23/07/25 - 04:21 AM: Moon with Alhena

* 23/07/25 - 11:02 AM: Mars with Denebola

* 23/07/25 - 12:46 PM: Moon with Sirius

* 23/07/25 - 02:18 PM: Moon with Canopus

* 23/07/25 - 02:21 PM: Venus with Bellatrix

* 23/07/25 - 11:17 PM: Moon with Castor

* 24/07/25 - 04:22 AM: Moon with Pollux

* 24/07/25 - 08:47 AM: Moon with Procyon

* 24/07/25 - 09:34 AM: Venus with Capella

* 24/07/25 - 11:33 AM: Mercury with Acubens

* 24/07/25 - 04:12 PM: Venus with Phact

* 25/07/25 - 12:35 AM: Venus with El Nath

* 25/07/25 - 04:02 PM: Moon with Acubens

* 25/07/25 - 07:04 PM: Venus with Alnilam

* 26/07/25 - 04:35 PM: Moon with Alphard

* 26/07/25 - 09:15 PM: Moon with Regulus

* 27/07/25 - 06:35 PM: Moon with Zosma

* 28/07/25 - 07:18 AM: Mars with Alkes

* 28/07/25 - 02:10 PM: Moon with Denebola

* 28/07/25 - 06:08 PM: Moon with Alkes

* 29/07/25 - 03:12 PM: Venus with Betelgeuse

* 29/07/25 - 11:58 PM: Moon with Diadem

* 30/07/25 - 01:55 AM: Moon with Vindemiatrix

* 31/07/25 - 05:41 AM: Moon with Spica

* 31/07/25 - 06:29 AM: Moon with Arcturus

AUGUST 2025 CONJUNCTIONS
All times given in UTC (Coordinated Universal Time)

* 01/08/25   - 07:00 PM: Moon with Alphecca

* 02/08/25   - 12:38 AM: Moon with Zuben Elgenubi

* 02/08/25   - 09:17 AM: Moon with Zuben Eschamali

* 02/08/25   - 06:12 PM: Moon with Agena

* 03/08/25   - 05:36 AM: Moon with Toliman

* 04/08/25   - 02:11 AM: Moon with Antares

* 04/08/25   - 02:47 PM: Moon with Ras Algethi

* 05/08/25   - 03:07 AM: Moon with Ras Alhague

* 05/08/25   - 09:36 AM: Moon with Aculeus

* 05/08/25   - 04:14 PM: Moon with Acumen

* 06/08/25   - 04:46 AM: Sun with Acubens

* 06/08/25   - 09:37 AM: Moon with Facies

* 06/08/25   - 03:58 PM: Venus with Mirzam (Al Murzims)

* 06/08/25   - 10:46 PM: Moon with Vega

* 07/08/25   - 01:15 AM: Moon with Rukbat

* 08/08/25   - 05:11 AM: Moon with Altair

* 08/08/25   - 07:21 AM: Venus with Alhena

* 09/08/25   - 09:13 AM: Moon with Sualocin

* 09/08/25   - 05:29 PM: Jupiter with Sirius

* 09/08/25   - 07:51 PM: Moon with Sadalsuud

* 09/08/25   - 08:06 PM: Moon with Deneb Algedi

* 10/08/25   - 01:17 PM: Moon with Sadalmelek

* 10/08/25 - 02:11 PM: Moon with Fomalhaut

* 10/08/25 - 04:42 PM: Moon with Deneb Adige

* 11/08/25 - 10:00 AM: Moon with Achernar

* 11/08/25 - 10:19 AM: Moon with Ankaa

* 11/08/25 - 07:01 PM: Venus with Sirius

* 12/08/25 - 12:01 AM: Moon with Markab

* 12/08/25 - 10:03 AM: Moon with Scheat

* 12/08/25 - 01:24 PM: Venus with Canopus

* 13/08/25 - 11:27 AM: Moon with Alpheraz

* 14/08/25 - 03:12 AM: Jupiter with Canopus

* 14/08/25 - 03:44 AM: Pluto with Altair

* 14/08/25 - 01:01 PM: Moon with Alrischa

* 14/08/25 - 02:39 PM: Moon with Mirach

* 15/08/25 - 02:53 AM: Moon with Hamal

* 15/08/25 - 03:05 AM: Moon with Schedir

* 15/08/25 - 02:08 PM: Moon with Menkar

* 16/08/25 - 06:45 AM: Moon with Capulus

* 16/08/25 - 10:07 AM: Moon with Algol

* 16/08/25 - 04:36 PM: Moon with Alcyone

* 16/08/25 - 08:07 PM: Moon with Mirfach

* 17/08/25 - 12:39 AM: Venus with Castor

* 17/08/25 - 09:12 AM: Moon with Aldebaran

* 17/08/25 - 09:10 PM: Moon with Rigel

* 18/08/25 - 04:11 AM: Moon with Bellatrix

* 18/08/25   - 05:45 AM: Moon with Capella
* 18/08/25   - 06:17 AM: Moon with Phact
* 18/08/25   - 06:58 AM: Moon with El Nath
* 18/08/25   - 08:29 AM: Moon with Alnilam
* 18/08/25   - 02:25 PM: Moon with Alkaid
* 18/08/25   - 05:34 PM: Moon with Betelgeuse
* 19/08/25   - 08:04 AM: Moon with Mirzam
* 19/08/25   - 11:23 AM: Moon with Alhena
* 19/08/25   - 12:48 PM: Venus with Pollux
* 19/08/25   - 08:00 PM: Moon with Sirius
* 19/08/25   - 09:34 PM: Moon with Canopus
* 20/08/25   - 06:45 AM: Moon with Castor
* 20/08/25   - 09:36 AM: Sun with Alphard
* 20/08/25   - 11:57 AM: Moon with Pollux
* 20/08/25   - 04:27 PM: Moon with Procyon
* 21/08/25   - 04:42 PM: Venus with Procyon
* 21/08/25   - 05:29 PM: Mars with Diadem
* 22/08/25   - 12:14 AM: Moon with Acubens
* 22/08/25   - 03:07 AM: Sun with Regulus
* 23/08/25   - 01:02 AM: Moon with Alphard
* 23/08/25   - 05:44 AM: Moon with Regulus
* 23/08/25   - 06:24 AM: Mars with Vindemiatrix
* 24/08/25   - 03:07 AM: Moon with Zosma
* 24/08/25   - 07:05 AM: Mercury with Acubens

* 24/08/25   - 10:40 PM: Moon with Denebola

* 25/08/25   - 02:37 AM: Moon with Alkes

* 26/08/25   - 08:16 AM: Moon with Diadem

* 26/08/25   - 10:12 AM: Moon with Vindemiatrix

* 27/08/25   - 01:47 PM: Moon with Spica

* 27/08/25   - 02:35 PM: Moon with Arcturus

* 29/08/25   - 02:05 AM: Moon with Acrux

* 29/08/25   - 02:58 AM: Moon with Alphecca

* 29/08/25   - 08:36 AM: Moon with Zuben Elgenubi

* 29/08/25   - 05:16 PM: Moon with Zuben Eschamali

* 30/08/25   - 02:13 AM: Moon with Agena

* 30/08/25   - 01:40 PM: Moon with Toliman

* 31/08/25   - 10:25 AM: Moon with Antares

* 31/08/25   - 11:09 PM: Moon with Ras Algethi

SEPTEMBER 2025 CONJUNCTIONS
All times given in UTC (Coordinated Universal Time)

* 01/09/25 - 07:27 AM: Mercury with Alphard

* 01/09/25 - 11:37 AM: Moon with Ras Alhague

* 01/09/25 - 06:11 PM: Moon with Aculeus

* 02/09/25 - 12:53 AM: Moon with Acumen

* 02/09/25 - 04:34 AM: Mercury with Regulus

* 02/09/25 - 06:29 PM: Moon with Facies

* 03/09/25 - 07:47 AM: Moon with Vega

* 03/09/25 - 10:18 AM: Moon with Rukbat

* 03/09/25 - 10:20 PM: Sun with Zosma

* 04/09/25 - 02:26 PM: Moon with Altair

* 05/09/25 - 07:54 AM: Saturn with Scheat

* 05/09/25 - 06:28 PM: Moon with Sualocin

* 06/09/25 - 05:02 AM: Moon with Sadalsuud

* 06/09/25 - 05:16 AM: Moon with Deneb Algedi

* 06/09/25 - 08:25 AM: Venus with Acubens

* 06/09/25 - 10:16 PM: Moon with Sadalmelek

* 06/09/25 - 11:09 PM: Moon with Fomalhaut

* 07/09/25 - 01:38 AM: Moon with Deneb Adige

* 07/09/25 - 06:38 PM: Moon with Achernar

* 07/09/25 - 06:56 PM: Moon with Ankaa

* 08/09/25 - 08:20 AM: Moon with Markab

* 08/09/25 - 02:16 PM: Mercury with Zosma

* 08/09/25 - 06:08 PM: Moon with Scheat

* 09/09/25 - 06:51 PM: Moon with Alpheraz

* 10/09/25 - 07:43 PM: Moon with Alrischa

* 10/09/25 - 09:18 PM: Moon with Mirach

* 11/09/25 - 09:14 AM: Moon with Hamal

* 11/09/25 - 09:25 AM: Moon with Schedir

* 11/09/25 - 06:54 PM: Jupiter with Castor

* 11/09/25 - 08:13 PM: Moon with Menkar

* 12/09/25 - 12:32 PM: Moon with Capulus

* 12/09/25 - 03:50 PM: Moon with Algol

* 12/09/25 - 09:09 PM: Mars with Arcturus

* 12/09/25 - 10:13 PM: Moon with Alcyone

* 13/09/25 - 01:42 AM: Moon with Mirfach

* 13/09/25 - 01:04 PM: Mercury with Denebola

* 13/09/25 - 02:39 PM: Moon with Aldebaran

* 13/09/25 - 02:40 PM: Mars with Spica

* 13/09/25 - 03:07 PM: Sun with Denebola

* 14/09/25 - 02:33 AM: Moon with Rigel

* 14/09/25 - 09:34 AM: Moon with Bellatrix

* 14/09/25 - 11:08 AM: Moon with Capella

* 14/09/25 - 11:40 AM: Moon with Phact

* 14/09/25 - 12:21 PM: Moon with El Nath

* 14/09/25 - 01:52 PM: Moon with Alnilam

* 14/09/25 - 07:49 PM: Moon with Alkaid

* 14/09/25   - 10:58 PM: Moon with Betelgeuse

* 15/09/25   - 03:14 AM: Mercury with Alkes

* 15/09/25   - 01:35 PM: Moon with Mirzam

* 15/09/25   - 04:56 PM: Moon with Alhena

* 16/09/25   - 01:39 AM: Moon with Sirius

* 16/09/25   - 03:14 AM: Moon with Canopus

* 16/09/25   - 12:32 PM: Moon with Castor

* 16/09/25   - 03:46 PM: Sun with Alkes

* 16/09/25   - 05:49 PM: Moon with Pollux

* 16/09/25   - 10:24 PM: Moon with Procyon

* 18/09/25   - 06:44 AM: Moon with Acubens

* 18/09/25   - 10:54 PM: Venus with Regulus

* 19/09/25   - 07:57 AM: Moon with Alphard

* 19/09/25   - 12:43 PM: Moon with Regulus

* 20/09/25   - 10:24 AM: Moon with Zosma

* 21/09/25   - 06:07 AM: Moon with Denebola

* 21/09/25   - 10:06 AM: Moon with Alkes

* 22/09/25   - 03:52 PM: Moon with Diadem

* 22/09/25   - 05:48 PM: Moon with Vindemiatrix

* 23/09/25   - 06:13 PM: Mercury with Diadem

* 23/09/25   - 09:22 PM: Moon with Spica

* 23/09/25   - 10:10 PM: Moon with Arcturus

* 24/09/25   - 08:09 AM: Mercury with Vindemiatrix

* 25/09/25   - 09:36 AM: Moon with Acrux

* 25/09/25 - 10:28 AM: Moon with Alphecca

* 25/09/25 - 04:06 PM: Moon with Zuben Elgenubi

* 26/09/25 - 12:46 AM: Moon with Zuben Eschamali

* 26/09/25 - 09:43 AM: Moon with Agena

* 26/09/25 - 09:12 PM: Moon with Toliman

* 27/09/25 - 06:05 PM: Moon with Antares

* 28/09/25 - 06:57 AM: Moon with Ras Algethi

* 28/09/25 - 07:35 PM: Moon with Ras Alhague

* 29/09/25 - 01:08 AM: Venus with Zosma

* 29/09/25 - 02:14 AM: Moon with Aculeus

* 29/09/25 - 09:02 AM: Moon with Acumen

* 30/09/25 - 02:58 AM: Moon with Facies

* 30/09/25 - 04:33 PM: Moon with Vega

* 30/09/25 - 07:07 PM: Moon with Rukbat

OCTOBER 2025 CONJUNCTIONS
All times given in UTC (Coordinated Universal Time)

* 01/10/25   - 11:50 PM: Moon with Altair

* 02/10/25   - 08:14 PM: Jupiter with Pollux

* 02/10/25   - 09:43 PM: Mercury with Spica

* 03/10/25   - 04:24 AM: Moon with Sualocin

* 03/10/25   - 03:08 PM: Moon with Sadalsuud

* 03/10/25   - 03:22 PM: Moon with Deneb Algedi

* 04/10/25   - 08:32 AM: Moon with Sadalmelek

* 04/10/25   - 09:26 AM: Moon with Fomalhaut

* 04/10/25   - 11:56 AM: Moon with Deneb Adige

* 05/10/25   - 04:58 AM: Moon with Achernar

* 05/10/25   - 05:16 AM: Moon with Ankaa

* 05/10/25   - 01:39 PM: Venus with Mirach

* 05/10/25   - 06:37 PM: Moon with Markab

* 06/10/25   - 04:20 AM: Moon with Scheat

* 06/10/25   - 04:30 PM: Venus with Denebola

* 07/10/25   - 04:38 AM: Moon with Alpheraz

* 08/10/25   - 04:53 AM: Moon with Alrischa

* 08/10/25   - 06:25 AM: Moon with Mirach

* 08/10/25   - 05:59 PM: Moon with Hamal

* 08/10/25   - 06:10 PM: Moon with Schedir

* 09/10/25   - 01:46 AM: Venus with Alkes

* 09/10/25   - 04:37 AM: Moon with Menkar

* 09/10/25 - 02:46 PM: Mars with Alphecca

* 09/10/25 - 08:23 PM: Moon with Capulus

* 09/10/25 - 11:35 PM: Moon with Algol

* 10/10/25 - 05:45 AM: Moon with Alcyone

* 10/10/25 - 06:55 AM: Mars with Acrux

* 10/10/25 - 09:08 AM: Moon with Mirfach

* 10/10/25 - 09:40 PM: Moon with Aldebaran

* 11/10/25 - 09:13 AM: Moon with Rigel

* 11/10/25 - 04:02 PM: Moon with Bellatrix

* 11/10/25 - 05:34 PM: Moon with Capella

* 11/10/25 - 06:06 PM: Moon with Phact

* 11/10/25 - 06:46 PM: Moon with El Nath

* 11/10/25 - 08:14 PM: Moon with Alnilam

* 12/10/25 - 02:02 AM: Moon with Alkaid

* 12/10/25 - 05:07 AM: Moon with Betelgeuse

* 12/10/25 - 07:27 PM: Moon with Mirzam

* 12/10/25 - 10:44 PM: Moon with Alhena

* 13/10/25 - 07:19 AM: Moon with Sirius

* 13/10/25 - 08:53 AM: Moon with Canopus

* 13/10/25 - 06:06 PM: Moon with Castor

* 13/10/25 - 11:19 PM: Moon with Pollux

* 14/10/25 - 03:53 AM: Moon with Procyon

* 14/10/25 - 07:00 PM: Mercury with Alphecca

* 14/10/25 - 09:51 PM: Mars with Zuben Elgenubi

* 15/10/25   - 12:13 PM: Moon with Acubens

* 16/10/25   - 01:37 PM: Moon with Alphard

* 16/10/25   - 06:26 PM: Moon with Regulus

* 17/10/25   - 11:01 AM: Mercury with Zuben Elgenubi

* 17/10/25   - 04:21 PM: Moon with Zosma

* 18/10/25   - 12:18 PM: Moon with Denebola

* 18/10/25   - 04:20 PM: Moon with Alkes

* 19/10/25   - 10:22 PM: Moon with Diadem

* 20/10/25   - 12:19 AM: Moon with Vindemiatrix

* 20/10/25   - 04:41 PM: Mercury with Zuben Eschamali

* 21/10/25   - 01:01 AM: Mars with Zuben Eschamali

* 21/10/25   - 04:02 AM: Moon with Spica

* 21/10/25   - 04:50 AM: Moon with Arcturus

* 21/10/25   - 08:53 AM: Venus with Diadem

* 22/10/25   - 03:50 AM: Venus with Vindemiatrix

* 22/10/25   - 04:19 PM: Moon with Acrux

* 22/10/25   - 05:11 PM: Moon with Alphecca

* 22/10/25   - 10:49 PM: Moon with Zuben Elgenubi

* 23/10/25   - 07:29 AM: Moon with Zuben Eschamali

* 23/10/25   - 04:25 PM: Moon with Agena

* 24/10/25   - 03:54 AM: Moon with Toliman

* 25/10/25   - 12:48 AM: Moon with Antares

* 25/10/25   - 01:43 PM: Moon with Ras Algethi

* 26/10/25   - 02:25 AM: Moon with Ras Alhague

* 26/10/25 - 09:07 AM: Moon with Aculeus
* 26/10/25 - 03:59 PM: Moon with Acumen
* 27/10/25 - 07:23 AM: Mars with Agena
* 27/10/25 - 10:10 AM: Moon with Facies
* 27/10/25 - 11:59 PM: Moon with Vega
* 28/10/25 - 02:36 AM: Moon with Rukbat
* 29/10/25 - 06:23 AM: Mercury with Toliman
* 29/10/25 - 08:01 AM: Moon with Altair
* 30/10/25 - 01:24 PM: Moon with Sualocin
* 31/10/25 - 12:27 AM: Moon with Sadalsuud
* 31/10/25 - 12:42 AM: Moon with Deneb Algedi
* 31/10/25 - 06:23 PM: Moon with Sadalmelek
* 31/10/25 - 07:18 PM: Moon with Fomalhaut
* 31/10/25 - 09:52 PM: Moon with Deneb Adige

NOVEMBER 2025 CONJUNCTIONS
All times given in UTC (Coordinated Universal Time)

* 01/11/25   - 03:21 PM: Moon with Achernar

* 01/11/25   - 03:40 PM: Moon with Ankaa

* 01/11/25   - 09:50 PM: Venus with Arcturus

* 02/11/25   - 05:18 AM: Moon with Markab

* 02/11/25   - 07:07 AM: Venus with Spica

* 02/11/25   - 12:57 PM: Mercury with Sadalmelek

* 02/11/25   - 03:11 PM: Moon with Scheat

* 03/11/25   - 03:44 PM: Moon with Alpheraz

* 03/11/25   - 10:41 PM: Sun with Alphecca

* 04/11/25   - 06:23 AM: Mars with Toliman

* 04/11/25   - 09:28 AM: Sun with Acrux

* 04/11/25   - 03:56 PM: Moon with Alrischa

* 04/11/25   - 05:28 PM: Moon with Mirach

* 04/11/25   - 07:27 PM: Neptune with Scheat

* 05/11/25   - 04:54 AM: Moon with Hamal

* 05/11/25   - 05:05 AM: Moon with Schedir

* 05/11/25   - 03:21 PM: Moon with Menkar

* 06/11/25   - 06:46 AM: Moon with Capulus

* 06/11/25   - 09:53 AM: Moon with Algol

* 06/11/25   - 03:53 PM: Moon with Alcyone

* 06/11/25   - 07:09 PM: Moon with Mirfach

* 07/11/25   - 07:18 AM: Moon with Aldebaran

* 07/11/25 - 02:29 PM: Sun with Zuben Elgenubi

* 07/11/25 - 06:28 PM: Moon with Rigel

* 08/11/25 - 01:03 AM: Moon with Bellatrix

* 08/11/25 - 02:31 AM: Moon with Capella

* 08/11/25 - 03:01 AM: Moon with Phact

* 08/11/25 - 03:40 AM: Moon with El Nath

* 08/11/25 - 05:05 AM: Moon with Alnilam

* 08/11/25 - 10:41 AM: Moon with Alkaid

* 08/11/25 - 01:39 PM: Moon with Betelgeuse

* 09/11/25 - 03:28 AM: Moon with Mirzam

* 09/11/25 - 06:39 AM: Moon with Alhena

* 09/11/25 - 02:56 PM: Moon with Sirius

* 09/11/25 - 04:27 PM: Moon with Canopus

* 09/11/25 - 04:38 PM: Mars with Sadalmelek

* 10/11/25 - 01:22 AM: Moon with Castor

* 10/11/25 - 06:26 AM: Moon with Pollux

* 10/11/25 - 10:51 AM: Moon with Procyon

* 11/11/25 - 06:24 PM: Moon with Acubens

* 11/11/25 - 08:50 PM: Sun with Zuben Eschamali

* 12/11/25 - 07:26 PM: Moon with Alphard

* 13/11/25 - 12:12 AM: Moon with Regulus

* 13/11/25 - 10:00 PM: Moon with Zosma

* 14/11/25 - 05:57 PM: Moon with Denebola

* 14/11/25 - 10:00 PM: Moon with Alkes

* 16/11/25 - 01:13 AM: Mercury with Sadalmelek
* 16/11/25 - 04:11 AM: Moon with Diadem
* 16/11/25 - 06:08 AM: Sun with Agena
* 16/11/25 - 06:08 AM: Moon with Vindemiatrix
* 16/11/25 - 07:58 AM: Venus with Alphecca
* 16/11/25 - 04:35 PM: Venus with Acrux
* 17/11/25 - 07:45 AM: Mars with Antares
* 17/11/25 - 10:01 AM: Moon with Spica
* 17/11/25 - 10:49 AM: Moon with Arcturus
* 17/11/25 - 02:07 PM: Venus with Alphard
* 18/11/25 - 06:38 AM: North Node with Ankaa
* 18/11/25 - 10:26 PM: Moon with Acrux
* 18/11/25 - 11:19 PM: Moon with Alphecca
* 19/11/25 - 04:57 AM: Moon with Zuben Elgenubi
* 19/11/25 - 06:02 AM: North Node with Achernar
* 19/11/25 - 06:04 AM: Venus with Zuben Elgenubi
* 19/11/25 - 06:53 AM: Mercury with Toliman
* 19/11/25 - 01:37 PM: Moon with Zuben Eschamali
* 19/11/25 - 10:33 PM: Moon with Agena
* 20/11/25 - 10:01 AM: Moon with Toliman
* 20/11/25 - 10:48 PM: Uranus with Alcyone
* 21/11/25 - 06:53 AM: Moon with Antares
* 21/11/25 - 07:45 PM: Moon with Ras Algethi
* 21/11/25 - 08:54 PM: Sun with Toliman

* 22/11/25   - 08:26 AM: Moon with Ras Alhague

* 22/11/25   - 03:07 PM: Moon with Aculeus

* 22/11/25   - 03:55 PM: Venus with Zuben Eschamali

* 22/11/25   - 09:58 PM: Moon with Acumen

* 23/11/25   - 04:11 PM: Moon with Facies

* 23/11/25   - 04:26 PM: Mercury with Agena

* 24/11/25   - 06:03 AM: Moon with Vega

* 24/11/25   - 08:41 AM: Moon with Rukbat

* 25/11/25   - 02:25 PM: Moon with Altair

* 25/11/25   - 05:29 PM: Sun with Sadalmelek

* 26/11/25   - 04:16 AM: Venus with Agena

* 26/11/25   - 08:23 PM: Moon with Sualocin

* 27/11/25   - 05:27 AM: Mars with Ras Algethi

* 27/11/25   - 07:44 AM: Moon with Sadalsuud

* 27/11/25   - 07:59 AM: Moon with Deneb Algedi

* 27/11/25   - 09:10 PM: Mars with Rukbat

* 28/11/25   - 02:13 AM: Moon with Sadalmelek

* 28/11/25   - 03:10 AM: Moon with Fomalhaut

* 28/11/25   - 05:50 AM: Moon with Deneb Adige

* 28/11/25   - 11:55 PM: Moon with Achernar

* 29/11/25   - 12:15 AM: Moon with Ankaa

* 29/11/25   - 02:23 PM: Moon with Markab

* 30/11/25   - 12:37 AM: Moon with Scheat

* 30/11/25   - 04:28 PM: Venus with Toliman

DECEMBER 2025 CONJUNCTIONS

All times given in UTC (Coordinated Universal Time)

* 01/12/25 - 02:01 AM: Moon with Alpheraz

* 01/12/25 - 04:40 AM: Sun with Antares

* 02/12/25 - 02:53 AM: Moon with Alrischa

* 02/12/25 - 04:27 AM: Moon with Mirach

* 02/12/25 - 04:06 PM: Moon with Hamal

* 02/12/25 - 04:17 PM: Moon with Schedir

* 03/12/25 - 02:42 AM: Moon with Menkar

* 03/12/25 - 06:14 PM: Moon with Capulus

* 03/12/25 - 06:55 PM: Venus with Sadalmelek

* 03/12/25 - 09:20 PM: Moon with Algol

* 04/12/25 - 03:21 AM: Moon with Alcyone

* 04/12/25 - 06:36 AM: Moon with Mirfach

* 04/12/25 - 06:40 PM: Moon with Aldebaran

* 05/12/25 - 05:41 AM: Moon with Rigel

* 05/12/25 - 12:09 PM: Moon with Bellatrix

* 05/12/25 - 01:36 PM: Moon with Capella

* 05/12/25 - 02:06 PM: Moon with Phact

* 05/12/25 - 02:44 PM: Moon with El Nath

* 05/12/25 - 04:07 PM: Moon with Alnilam

* 05/12/25 - 05:14 PM: Mars with Ras Alhague

* 05/12/25 - 09:36 PM: Moon with Alkaid

* 06/12/25 - 12:30 AM: Moon with Betelgeuse

* 06/12/25 - 01:02 PM: Mercury with Agena

* 06/12/25 - 01:57 PM: Moon with Mirzam

* 06/12/25 - 05:02 PM: Moon with Alhena

* 07/12/25 - 01:04 AM: Moon with Sirius

* 07/12/25 - 02:32 AM: Moon with Canopus

* 07/12/25 - 11:09 AM: Moon with Castor

* 07/12/25 - 04:03 PM: Moon with Pollux

* 07/12/25 - 08:19 PM: Moon with Procyon

* 08/12/25 - 04:30 AM: Venus with Antares

* 08/12/25 - 08:38 AM: Sun with Ras Algethi

* 08/12/25 - 08:03 PM: Sun with Rukbat

* 09/12/25 - 02:47 AM: Moon with Acubens

* 10/12/25 - 03:02 AM: Moon with Alphard

* 10/12/25 - 04:15 AM: Mars with Aculeus

* 10/12/25 - 07:40 AM: Moon with Regulus

* 11/12/25 - 01:43 AM: Pluto with Altair

* 11/12/25 - 04:55 AM: Moon with Zosma

* 11/12/25 - 06:41 PM: Mercury with Toliman

* 12/12/25 - 12:30 AM: Moon with Denebola

* 12/12/25 - 04:29 AM: Moon with Alkes

* 13/12/25 - 10:22 AM: Moon with Diadem

* 13/12/25 - 12:19 PM: Moon with Vindemiatrix

* 13/12/25 - 11:07 PM: Venus with Ras Algethi

* 14/12/25   - 02:26 AM: Mars with Acumen

* 14/12/25   - 08:20 AM: Venus with Rukbat

* 14/12/25   - 01:25 PM: Sun with Ras Alhague

* 14/12/25   - 04:07 PM: Moon with Spica

* 14/12/25   - 04:55 PM: Moon with Arcturus

* 14/12/25   - 08:00 PM: Mercury with Sadalmelek

* 16/12/25   - 04:36 AM: Moon with Acrux

* 16/12/25   - 05:29 AM: Moon with Alphecca

* 16/12/25   - 11:07 AM: Moon with Zuben Elgenubi

* 16/12/25   - 07:49 PM: Moon with Zuben Eschamali

* 17/12/25   - 04:46 AM: Moon with Agena

* 17/12/25   - 04:14 PM: Moon with Toliman

* 17/12/25   - 08:01 PM: Sun with Aculeus

* 18/12/25   - 01:04 PM: Moon with Antares

* 18/12/25   - 08:45 PM: Mercury with Antares

* 18/12/25   - 11:15 PM: Venus with Ras Alhague

* 19/12/25   - 01:54 AM: Moon with Ras Algethi

* 19/12/25   - 02:31 PM: Moon with Ras Alhague

* 19/12/25   - 09:10 PM: Moon with Aculeus

* 20/12/25   - 03:59 AM: Moon with Acumen

* 20/12/25   - 05:46 PM: Sun with Acumen

* 20/12/25   - 10:04 PM: Moon with Facies

* 21/12/25   - 06:20 AM: Jupiter with Pollux

* 21/12/25   - 11:50 AM: Moon with Vega

* 21/12/25 - 02:27 PM: Moon with Rukbat

* 21/12/25 - 02:48 PM: Venus with Aculeus

* 22/12/25 - 08:00 PM: Moon with Altair

* 23/12/25 - 09:36 PM: Mercury with Ras Algethi

* 23/12/25 - 11:24 PM: Venus with Acumen

* 24/12/25 - 01:58 AM: Moon with Sualocin

* 24/12/25 - 05:29 AM: Mercury with Rukbat

* 24/12/25 - 01:23 PM: Moon with Sadalsuud

* 24/12/25 - 01:38 PM: Moon with Deneb Algedi

* 25/12/25 - 08:04 AM: Moon with Sadalmelek

* 25/12/25 - 09:01 AM: Moon with Fomalhaut

* 25/12/25 - 11:43 AM: Moon with Deneb Adige

* 26/12/25 - 06:09 AM: Moon with Achernar

* 26/12/25 - 06:29 AM: Moon with Ankaa

* 26/12/25 - 05:54 PM: Mars with Facies

* 26/12/25 - 08:59 PM: Moon with Markab

* 27/12/25 - 07:31 AM: Moon with Scheat

* 28/12/25 - 03:18 AM: Mercury with Ras Alhague

* 28/12/25 - 09:48 AM: Moon with Alpheraz

* 29/12/25 - 11:37 AM: Moon with Alrischa

* 29/12/25 - 01:15 PM: Moon with Mirach

* 30/12/25 - 01:20 AM: Moon with Hamal

* 30/12/25 - 01:32 AM: Moon with Schedir

* 30/12/25 - 03:19 AM: Sun with Facies

* 30/12/25   - 08:20 AM: Mercury with Aculeus
* 30/12/25   - 12:20 PM: Moon with Menkar
* 31/12/25   - 04:23 AM: Moon with Capulus
* 31/12/25   - 07:36 AM: Moon with Algol
* 31/12/25   - 01:47 PM: Moon with Alcyone
* 31/12/25   - 07:36 AM: Moon with Algol
* 31/12/25   - 01:47 PM: Moon with Alcyone
* 31/12/25   - 01:48 PM: Venus with Facies
* 31/12/25   - 05:08 PM: Moon with Mirfach

REFERENCES AND FURTHER READING

Astrology Software: Solar Fire V9, Astrolabe Inc, 2019

Bernadette Brady. "Brady's Book of Fixed Stars". Samuel Weiser Inc. ,York Beach ME, 1998

Bernadette Brady, Chloe Margherita. "Brady's Book of Fixed Stars: The Invisible Force and Influence of Constellations in the Natal Chart". Weiser Classics Series, 2024.

Diana K. Rosenberg . "Secrets of the Ancient Skies", Vol 1 & 2, Ancient Skies Press

D.M. Hoover. "Exploring Critical Degrees and the Fixed Stars". 2017.

Ebertin-Hoffman. "Fixed Stars and their Interpretation". 2009.

Elizabeth M Hazel, Michael Munkasey. "The Little Book of Fixed Stars: Expanded Second Edition", 2020.

George C Noonan. "Fixed Stars and Judicial Astrology". 2009.

L.H. Weston. "The Fixed Stars in Astrology". 2007.

Oscar Hoffman. "Fixed Stars in the Chart: Constellations, Lunar Mansions and Mythology." 2019

Regulus Hess, Christopher Warnock. "De Quindecim Stellis: The Comprehensive Translations of Hermes on the Fifteen Fixed Stars". 2022.

Vivian Robson. "The Fixed Stars and Constellations in Astrology". Cecil Palmer, London, 1920

NOTES